Legal

KEYS

KEYBOARDING DRILLS & TERMINOLOGY

Jennie Bedford

Copp Clark Pitman Ltd.
A Longman Company
Toronto

ISBN 0-7730-5032-9

Editing: June Trusty
Design: Zena Denchik
Printing and Binding: Alger Press

Canadian Cataloguing in Publication Data

Bedford, Jennie
  Legal keys : keyboarding drills and terminology

ISBN 0-7730-5032-9

1. Electronic data processing — Keyboarding — Problems, exercises, etc.   2. Legal secretaries — Handbooks, manuals, etc.   I. Title.

KE355.A96B4 1991   652.3'26   C90-095695-X
KF320.A9B4 1991

For Doug, without whose support this book would not have been possible

Copp Clark Pitman Ltd.
2775 Matheson Boulevard East
Mississauga, Ontario
L4W 4P7

Written, printed, and bound in Canada

CONTENTS

PREFACE

Students wanting to enter law-related fields are confronted with a new language, "legalese," which features numerous Latin terms, long words, and sentences that never seem to end — or even make sense! Despite their interest in the law, many students shy away from law courses because they think they cannot learn all the legal terms. This is why *Legal Keys* has been written. This textbook aims to demystify the strange world of legalese through the medium of keyboarding drills, timed writings, and production exercises. In addition, the text introduces you to the concepts of discipline, ethical behaviour, confidentiality, and accuracy that are of paramount importance in law-related careers. *Legal Keys* introduces you to a variety of areas of law and the associated terminology. It is hoped that you will find law and legal secretarial courses more interesting and easier to comprehend as a result of the hands-on applications provided in this text.

The following is a prime example of the difference between everyday language and legalese:

If one person were to give another person an orange, he or she would simply say: "Have an orange."

When the transaction is entrusted to a lawyer to be put in writing, he or she uses this form:

"I hereby give and convey to you, all and singular, my estate and interest, right, title, claim, and advantage of and in the said orange, together with all its rind, skin, juice, pulp, and pips, and all rights and advantages therein, with full power to bite, cut, suck, and otherwise eat the same or give the same away with or without the rind, skin, juice, pulp, or pips, anything hereinbefore or hereinafter or in any other means of whatever nature or kind whatsoever to the contrary in any wise notwithstanding."

And then another lawyer comes along and takes the orange away!

–Source unknown.

INTRODUCTION

Audience

Legal Keys is designed for use by students who have keyboarding experience, whether on a typewriter, word processor, or computer. The material presented in the drills will be of special interest to those students who want to enter law-related occupations, as well as those who just want to learn more about law as a life skill.

Purpose

The main purpose for using *Legal Keys* is to:
- Develop expertise in keying legal material.
- Expand knowledge of legal terms, documents, and procedures.

Emphasis

The main emphasis of *Legal Keys* is on accurate, rhythmic keying. While keyboarding speed is important, speed without accuracy has no place in law-related occupations, where errors can result in costly law suits, loss of clients, etc.

Legal Keys emphasizes:
- Reading and comprehending material before it is keyed.
- Setting performance goals.
- Conducting self-evaluation of progress.
- Using a dictionary and office handbook.

Content

Legal Keys has 100% Canadian content. Legal documentation and procedures vary from province to province; therefore, every effort has been made to provide generic materials so that this text can be used by students across Canada. The drills, timed writings, and production practice exercises are presented in both keyed and handwritten format and cover a wide variety of topics, from the court system, to conveyancing and contract law. As you already have keyboarding skills, the drills and timings are not contrived in any way. The material presented is, therefore, interesting and informative.

Organization

Legal Keys is divided into six units, each of which is devoted to one area of law. Each unit is self-contained, so you can work on the units in any order.

The drills and timings in each unit increase in length and difficulty as you work through the unit. Each unit is organized as follows:

Word practice	(20 words)
Phrase practice	(10 phrases)
One-minute timings	(5 timings)
Comprehension 1	(6 sentences)
Sentence practice	(12 sentences)
Two-minute timings	(4 timings)
Comprehension 2	(10 words)
Paragraph practice	(6 paragraphs)
Three-minute timings	(3 timings)
Comprehension 3	(12 sentences)
Five- or ten-minute timings	(3 timings)
Production exercises	(3 exercises)

Accuracy drills include word, phrase, sentence, and paragraph practice. They provide students with an opportunity to practise keying the legal terminology presented in the timed writings that follow.

A large selection of timed writings is provided in each unit: one-minute, two-minute, three-minute, and five- or ten-minute. These timings are of adequate length to challenge students who have a high keyboarding speed. They give all students ample opportunity to practise both keyboarding speed and accuracy.

The "Comprehension 1" section that follows the one-minute timings presents a series of sentences related to the preceding timed writings, but with the legal terminology missing. You are required to fill in the missing legal terms.

"Comprehension 2," which follows the two-minute timings, presents a series of words that you must put into a sentence of your own composition. You are encouraged to use a dictionary.

"Comprehension 3," which follows the three-minute timings, presents a series of sentences containing misused and misspelled words, as well as incorrect grammar, punctuation, and capitalization. You are required to locate the errors and key the sentences correctly.

The production exercises section, which follows the five- or ten-minute timings, provides you with an opportunity to produce generic legal correspondence and documentation. These production exercises incorporate legal terms from the preceding drills and timings in the unit and are designed to encourage you to use your common sense and initiative.

Setting Goals and Evaluating Progress

Throughout *Legal Keys*, you are encouraged to take the initiative to set your own speed and accuracy goals and to evaluate your progress.

Calculating Keyboarding Speed

To calculate gross words per minute, read the number in the right-hand, vertical, word-count column that corresponds to the last complete line of keyed material. For any part-line of keyed material, read the number along the horizontal scale at the

foot of the timing. Add the two numbers together and divide by the number of minutes of inputting.

Where applicable in handwritten timings, five-space paragraph indentations should be used. Since no horizontal scale is provided, part-lines are calculated by counting each character and space keyed in the part-line and then dividing the total by five.

Keyboarding Tips for Computer Users

All of the materials in *Legal Keys* are designed for students using typewriters, word processors, or computers. Students using computers are encouraged to use whatever features will assist them in producing good-quality, accurate work. This includes using spellchecks, adding words to custom (legal) dictionaries, correcting errors, writing macros (storing keystrokes), etc. All work should be stored and backed-up diskettes prepared at the end of each work session.

INDEX

Our
Legal System

SIGNED, PUBLISHED AND DECLARED)
by the said CECILIA ROSEMARY)
HINDS as and for a Codicil to)
his Last Will and Testament,)
in the presence of us, both)
present at the same time, who,)
at his request, in his)
presence, and in the presence)
of each other have hereunto)
subscribed our names as)
witnesses:)

_____
Name

_____
Address

_____   _____
                                                    CELIA ROSEMARY HINDS

_____
Occupation

_____
Name

_____
Address

_____

_____
Occupation

Note: At least two lines of Clause 1 and the remainder of the Codicil (including the attestation) should be on the final page.

WORD PRACTICE

Key one line of each of the following words. Concentrate on accuracy and rhythmic keying.

law	court
civil	judiciary
criminal	Parliament
common	justice
rule	advocated
precedent	independence
codification	statute
Code	society
Judge	decisions
case	legal

PHRASE PRACTICE

Key each of the following phrases six times. Concentrate on accuracy. Say each phrase to yourself as you key it. Remember to key rhythmically.

rule of precedent	Roman law
stare decisis	independence of the judiciary
common law system	legal decisions
criminal law	case law
French Civil Code	precedent-setting cases

EXERCISE 3

Read the following Codicil, watching for errors, and follow the instructions carefully. Set yourself a production time limit and then key the document quickly and accurately.

THIS IS A CODICIL TO THE LAST WILL AND TESTAMENT of me, CELIA ROSEMARY HINDS, Electrician, of 1784 Water Street, in the Town of Yarmouth in the Province of Nova Scotia, which Last Will and Testament bears date the 18th day November, 1974.

(Celia wants to revoke paragraph 9.0 of her Will. Use the wording in Clause 6 on page 185, including the names of the guardians shown there.)

2.   In all other respects I confirm my said Will.

IN TESTIMONY WHEREOF I have to this Codicil to my Last Will and Testament, subscribed my name this   day of   , 19--.

1-MINUTE TIMINGS

Read the following paragraphs carefully. Set your speed and accuracy goals. Take a one-minute timing on each paragraph.

TIMING 1

The term "law" has many different definitions: a means of	12
protecting society; a reflection of society's current values	24
and beliefs; a set of rules that can be enforced by the	35
courts; a means of solving social problems; a method by	46
which people achieve justice in society; and a general term	58
for Acts/Statutes and Regulations. There is no one standard	70
definition of law.	74

. . . . 1 . . . . 2 . . . . 3 . . . . 4 . . . . 5 . . . . 6 . . . . 7 . . . . 8 . . . . 9 . . . .10 . . . .11 12

TIMING 2

The origins of Canadian law lie in the two main nations that	12
influenced settlement in Canada: France and Great Britain.	24
The systems of law in these two countries were very differ-	36
ent. The French legal system was based on Roman law, which	48
advocated codification of laws and law-making by the monar-	60
chy. The British legal system, however, was based on	71
unwritten customs and the monarchy was not involved in the	83
law-making process.	87

. . . . 1 . . . . 2 . . . . 3 . . . . 4 . . . . 5 . . . . 6 . . . . 7 . . . . 8 . . . . 9 . . . .10 . . . .11 12

Read the following portion of the Executrix's accounts. Check the accounts for accuracy and calculate the appropriate totals. Set yourself a production time limit and then key the accounts quickly and accurately.

ESTATE OF SHIRLEY PAULINE BATTISTA, DECEASED

SCHEDULE II

CAPITOL RECEIPTS

19--

Jan. 15	Funds to pay nursing accounts (Bank of Montreal account)	$ 598.00
Feb. 2	Funds to pay for funeral (Bank of Montreal account)	8,540,42
Apr. 2	Proceeds of Royale Bank deposit	20,619.22
Apr. 5	Proceeds of Maritime Trust account	1,594.39
May. 12	Part proceeds of Prairie Trust term deposit	5,000
June 4	Richardson Industries--Pension	435.67
Aug 30	Proceeds of Prairie Trust term term deposit	9,000.00
	TOTAL CASH RECIEPTS	
	ADD: VALUE OF SECURTIES	$59,873.21
	TOTAL	$

I hereby approve the Accounts of the Executrix as contained in this page and attached pages, approve the statement of distribution, and waive formal passing of the same:

_____
NAOMI ANDREA HUROWITZ

TIMING 3

Two major influences of Roman law were codification and the   12
use of Latin terms. Codification is the organization of   23
law into numbered volumes, based on the topic of law. The   35
influence of the French legal system can be seen in Quebec   47
today, where Judges use the French Civil Code (based on   58
codification) as the basis for legal decision-making.   69
This contrasts with English-speaking Canada, where decisions   81
are based on British common law.   87

. . . .1. . . .2. . . .3. . . .4. . . .5. . . .6. . . .7. . . .8. . . .9. . . .10. . . .11. . . .12

TIMING 4

Under the British common law system, Judges make   10
decisions based on the rule of precedent or stare decisis   22
(standing by previously decided cases). This means that   33
similar cases are treated alike. A Judge in a lower court   45
bases decisions on the precedents set by courts at the   56
same level or higher. Precedents can be overturned   66
only by a Judge sitting in a higher court or by the   76
passing of a new statute.   81

TIMING 5

Another inheritance from Great Britain is the independence   12
of the judiciary (Judges). Although some Judges are ap-   23
pointed by federal and provincial governments, they make   34

. . . .1. . . .2. . . .3. . . .4. . . .5. . . .6. . . .7. . . .8. . . .9. . . .10. . . .11. . . .12

PRODUCTION EXERCISES

EXERCISE 1

Read the following "Notice to Creditors and Others," watching for errors. Set yourself a production time limit and then key the Notice quickly and accurately. Box the Notice.

NOTICE TO CREDITORS AND OTHERS

IN THE ESTATE OF YUET YOK YEE, DECEASED

All persons having claims against the Estate of YUET YOK YEE (a.k.a. YEE YUET YOK), late of Moose Jaw Saskatchewan, who died on or about June 4, 19--, are hereby notified to send particulars of same to the undersigned Administrator at 106 Admiral Crescent, Moose Jaw, Saskatchewan S7H 1N5 on or beofre the 31th day of August, 19--, after which date the Estate will be distributed, with regard only to the claims of which the undersigned shall then have notice, and the undersigned will not be liable to any person of whose cliam they shall not then have notice.

DATED at Moose Jaw, Saskathewan, this 14th day of July, 19--.

PHILIP LEUNG
ANDREW GEORGE

Administrators

FINGOLD, CHONG & CO.

Solicitors

legal decisions based on case law (reports of precedent-setting cases) and statutes, not the wishes of government officials. Further independence of the judiciary is effected by Judges not being allowed to vote in elections or express political opinions.

	45
	56
	66
	77
	83

`....1....2....3....4....5....6....7....8....9....10....11....12`

Did you achieve your speed and accuracy goals on at least one of the timings? If not, repeat the timings.

COMPREHENSION 1

Key the following sentences once, filling in each blank with the appropriate legal term or phrase.

1. The French legal system was based on --- law.

2. --- is the organization of law into numbered volumes, based on the topic of law.

3. In Quebec, Judges use the --- as the basis for legal decision-making.

4. Under the British common law system, Judges make decisions based on the rule of --- or --- (Latin term).

5. Another inheritance from Great Britain is the independence of the ---.

6. Precedents can be overturned only by a --- sitting in a higher court or by the passing of a new ---.

Check your answers with your instructor.

is called "distributing the estate" or "distribution"), he or she should prepare a Release and send a copy of the Executor's or Administrator's accounts. The beneficiaries or heirs-at-law should review the accounts carefully and, if they agree with the accounting, sign the Release forms to indicate their agreement. This releases the Executor or Administrator from any further liability. In other words, a beneficiary cannot come back three years later and claim that the Executor or Administrator did not distribute a gift to him or her. If the beneficiaries or heirs-at-law do not agree with the accounting, they can request the Court Registrar to review the accounts. This process is usually referred to as a "passing of accounts." Once the Registrar is satisfied with the accounts, the beneficiaries or heirs-at-law sign the Releases and the estate is wound-up.

In some provinces, if an estate is small, no applications for Grants have to be made to the court; however, the transmission and distribution procedures are the same.

If an estate is very large or someone is contesting the validity or wording of a Will, the obtaining of the Grants, or the valuation of the estate, the transmission and distribution procedures can take months or even years to complete.

Read the following sentences carefully. Key each sentence once.
Concentrate on accuracy and rhythmic keying.

1. Our criminal laws are set out in the Criminal Code of Canada, which applies to all Canadians, irrespective of the province or territory in which they reside.

2. Criminal law covers all of the crimes set out in the Criminal Code of Canada as well as certain federal laws that are not covered in the Criminal Code; for example, the Narcotic Control Act.

3. The penalty for committing a crime is punishment: either imprisonment or a fine.

4. When someone commits a crime, he or she will be tried by the state (the Crown).

5. Civil law embodies all areas of law other than those set out in the Criminal Code of Canada or those that are designated as criminal law.

6. Civil law is codified only in Quebec (The Civil Code of the Province of Quebec); all other areas of Canada follow the British common law system.

7. Civil law includes matters relating to property, contracts, and torts.

8. A tort is a wrongdoing against a person or property.

9. Civil lawsuits seek compensation, whereas criminal proceedings seek punishment.

deceased are transferred into the name of the Executor or Administrator, or directly into the names of the beneficiaries. The process of transferring assets is known as "transmission."

Before assets can be transmitted, the institution or party holding the deceased's assets will require the law firm to provide certain documentation. For example, most banks will not release monies from the deceased's bank account without first seeing a certified copy of the Death Certificate and a copy of the Grant. Some institutions require a notarially certified copy of the Grant. This means that the lawyer must append a Notarial Certificate to a copy of the Grant.

When stocks and bonds are to be transmitted, the various companies and institutions involved will advise the law firm of the documentation they require. Most companies will accept a Declaration of Transmission and the Share Certificate. Often the transmission documentation has to be sent to the Transfer Agent for the company, so that new shares can be issued. When Canada Savings Bonds are to be transmitted, two special Bank of Canada Transfer Forms must be completed.

When the Executor or Administrator transmits the gifts to the beneficiaries or heirs-at-law (which

10. Civil lawsuits involve individuals and/or corporations, not the state.

11. International law consists of the treaties that various countries of the world have signed, which have been accepted as being legally binding on all nations.

12. Matters relating to international law may be heard in the World Court located in The Hague, the Netherlands.

2-MINUTE TIMINGS

Read the following paragraphs carefully. Set your speed and accuracy goals. Take a two-minute timing on each paragraph.

TIMING 1

There are many different classifications of law. Criminal	12
law, as the name implies, relates to crimes committed	23
under the Criminal Code. Civil law relates to non-	33
criminal matters such as property, contracts, and torts.	44
Constitutional law governs the relations within and	54
between the federal and provincial governments in	64
Canada. Statute law relates to the laws (statutes or	75
Acts) passed by the federal government and the	84
provincial legislatures. Administrative law relates to	95
the various regulations and regulatory bodies that	105

Investigations should be made to find out whether anyone | 428
owed the deceased any money--look specifically for | 438
Promissory Notes--or whether the deceased owed anyone | 449
else money. Look for bills from hospitals, funeral homes, | 461
utilities (telephone and hydro), and credit card companies. | 473

Finally, you should check with Canada Pension for death | 484
benefits and survivors benefits. | 490

. . . .1. . . .2. . . .3. . . .4. . . .5. . . .6. . . .7. . . .8. . . .9. . . .10. . . .11. . . .12

TIMING 3 (5 or 10 min)

The law firm submits a certified copy of the Death | 10
Certificate, the original Will (if there is one), a copy | 21
of the Certificate confirming the Wills search, various | 32
Notices and Affidavits, and fees to the court, and | 42
asks for the Executor's appointment to be confirmed | 52
or the Administrator to be appointed, the Will to be | 62
probated, and an appropriate Grant issued. | 70

Once the law firm has received the appropriate | 79
Grant from the court, a "Notice to Creditors and | 89
Others" is published several times in a local | 98
newspaper as well as the provincial Gazette. | 107
This Notice gives creditors 21 days to contact the | 117
Executor or Administrator, care of the law firm. | 127
As soon as this time period has expired, the | 136
debts of the estate are paid and the assets of the | 146

are often established to administer a statute or Act passed by a government. Military law incorporates the laws that relate to military personnel only. The military must also abide by the laws of Canada.

115
123
132
141
145

TIMING 2

When cases are tried before a court, the cases and the
parties involved must be identified. The reason for this
is that, under common law, a Judge trying another case
must base his or her judgment (in the absence of statute
law) on the rule of precedent or stare decisis. Cases are
identified by means of citations. For example, a citation
of a criminal case would be R. v. Mouritsen. The "R."
is an abbreviation for the Latin term "Regina" meaning
"queen" or "Rex" meaning "king." So R. v. Mouritsen
means that this is a criminal case in which the Crown
brought an individual named Mouritsen into court to face
criminal charges. An example of a citation for a civil
litigation case would be Petrovich v. XYZ Company Ltd. This
means that someone named Petrovich is suing XYZ Company Ltd.

11
22
33
44
56
68
79
90
100
111
122
133
145
157

. . . . 1 . . . . 2 . . . . 3 . . . . 4 . . . . 5 . . . 6 . . . . 7 . . . . 8 . . . . 9 . . . . 10 . . . . 11 12

All assets must be assigned a value as at the date of
death. In the case of household goods and furniture, paintings, jewellery, cars, and boats, professional evaluations
have to be prepared. Real estate has to be valued (both
market and assessed value) and outstanding mortgage balances
obtained.

Insurance policies must be located and the insurance companies contacted to confirm the names of the beneficiaries
and to determine what documentation the insurance company
requires to pay-out the beneficiaries. If the estate is
the beneficiary, the value of the insurance policy must be
included in the schedule of assets. If a beneficiary (other
than the estate) is named, then the insurance policy value
is not included in the estate valuation.

Employers of the deceased have to be contacted to obtain
information on any pensions, group life insurance, salary,
holiday pay, etc. If the deceased was self-employed or
had any business interests, you will have to contact the
deceased's accountant and work with him or her in ascertain-
ing the value of such business interests.

If the deceased held any stocks or bonds (often found in a
safety deposit box), these should be valued (as at the date
of death) by a stockbroker. You should not rely on newspaper stock prices because these are sometimes inaccurate.

TIMING 3

Constitutional law relates to the operations of both the   11

federal and provincial governments as set out in the   21

Constitution Act, 1982. This Act contains a number of   32

important statutes, including the British North America Act   44

1867 (now known as the Constitution Act, 1867). The British   56

North America Act, enacted by the British Parliament,   67

created the Dominion of Canada and outlined the powers of   78

the federal and provincial governments. As a result, Canada   90

inherited a Constitution similar to the British one. This   102

was a problem because it gave the two levels of Canadian   113

government absolute power to create laws and modify the   124

common law. The Canadian Charter of Rights and Freedoms,   135

1982, changed this absolute power; now the courts can   146

challenge legislation as being unconstitutional under the   157

Charter. Any disputes relating to the Constitution are   168

heard in the Supreme Court of Canada, the highest court in   180

the country.   182

. . . . 1 . . . . 2 . . . . 3 . . . . 4 . . . . 5 . . . . 6 . . . . 7 . . . . 8 . . . . 9 . . . . 10 . . . . 11 12

TIMING 4

For the Canadian common law legal system to function prop-   12

erly, it is essential that Judges and lawyers know about   23

precedent-setting cases. These cases are, therefore,   34

reported in case law reports. Some of the most common   45

. . . . 1 . . . . 2 . . . . 3 . . . . 4 . . . . 5 . . . . 6 . . . . 7 . . . . 8 . . . . 9 . . . . 10 . . . . 11 12

government official). |375|

Many provinces have Wills Variation Acts, which allow |386|
surviving spouses and children to apply to the court for a |398|
variation of a Will when little or no provision has been |409|
made for them to benefit. Notices should be sent to these |421|
people to inform them of their right to apply under any |432|
such Acts. Many provinces also require Notices to be sent |444|
to common law spouses and illegitimate children. |454|

· · · ·1· · · ·2· · · ·3· · · ·4· · · ·5· · · ·6· · · ·7· · · ·8· · · ·9· · · ·10· · · ·11· · · ·12

TIMING 2 (5 or 10 min)

One of the major jobs to be done on any estate is the prep- |12|
aration of a schedule of assets and liabilities of the |23|
deceased. Considerable time and effort must be expended to |35|
obtain this information: no stone must remain unturned! |46|
The task is often assigned to senior legal secretaries or |57|
legal assistants/paralegals/law clerks. |65|

To obtain the required information, you must locate the |76|
deceased's cheque books, account passbooks, bank statements, |88|
tax returns, insurance policies, real estate documents, etc. |100|
You will be required to write to banks, trust companies, |111|
credit unions, insurance companies, securities brokers, etc., |123|
to obtain information on bank accounts, safety deposit boxes, |135|
money on deposit, Registered Retirement Savings Plans, |146|
insurance policies, and investments (stocks and bonds). |157|

· · · ·1· · · ·2· · · ·3· · · ·4· · · ·5· · · ·6· · · ·7· · · ·8· · · ·9· · · ·10· · · ·11· · · ·12

case law reports are Dominion Law Reports (D.L.R.), Western | 57
Weekly Reports (W.W.R.), Canadian Criminal Cases (C.C.C.), | 68
Criminal Reports (C.R.), Supreme Court Reports (S.C.R.), | 79
and Reports of Family Law (R.F.L.). Case law reports are | 90
published in volumes that are organized chronologically. | 101
Each case law report has a specific citation; for example, | 113
Zwicker v. Levy [1955] 3 D.L.R. 718. If you looked on | 124
page 718 of the third volume of the Dominion Law Reports for | 136
1955, you would find the case law report relating to the | 147
Zwicker v. Levy case. | 151

. . . .1. . . .2. . . .3. . . .4. . . .5. . . .6. . . .7. . . .8. . . .9. . . .10. . . .11. . . .12

COMPREHENSION 2

Indicate your knowledge of the following terms by using each one in a separate sentence. If you are uncertain of any words, use your dictionary.

criminal law	military law
civil law	Regina
statute law	citation
constitutional law	case law reports
international law	Criminal Code

PARAGRAPH PRACTICE

Read the following paragraphs and then key an accurate copy of each. If you make any errors, drill each word correctly for one minute.

takes unnecessary risks or makes stupid mistakes that result in a loss to the estate, he or she can be held personally liable for rectifying the loss.

If your law firm is acting on behalf of an Executor or Administrator, the following things must be done.

1. A thorough search must be made for a Will and a Wills search conducted in your provincial Vital Statistics Department. A certificate that shows the results of a Wills Search will have to be submitted to the court.

2. Certified copies of the Death Certificate must be obtained from your provincial Vital Statistics Department.

3. The names and addresses of the beneficiaries or heirs-at-law must be obtained. If there is a Will, most provincial statutes require that a Notice plus a copy of the Will be sent to each beneficiary. If there is no Will, usually a Notice stating the name of the person wanting to apply to the Court to be an Administrator must be sent to the heirs-at-law.

While provincial procedures and Acts vary, it is normal for Notices intended for minors to be sent to the child's parent or guardian and to the Public Trustee or Official Guardian (or similar government official). Notices intended for the mentally incompetent are mailed to the Committee and to the Public Trustee or Official Guardian (or similar

PARAGRAPH 1

Law can be defined as a reflection of our society's current
beliefs and attitudes; however, the law often lags behind
the cutting edge of new ideologies. As beliefs and
attitudes change, society places pressure on governments to
change the law. This pressure may be in the form of
individuals or special interest groups lobbying MPs or MLAs,
media exposure, demonstrations, and sometimes civil
disobedience.

PARAGRAPH 2

Pressure from individuals or special interest groups could
lead to the federal or a provincial government enacting
legislation (making new laws). Alternatively, the
government involved may set up a parliamentary committee or
sub-committee or a Royal Commission to examine the concerns
being expressed by the public. These committees and Royal
Commissions prepare reports that they submit to the federal
or provincial government. Federal and provincial Law Reform
Commissions are established to review legislation and case
law and to make recommendations regarding the repeal
(abolition) or amendment of existing laws or the enactment
of new laws.

10.	The Executor predeceased her.

11.	The duties of an Executor and an Adminstrator are not the same.

12.	The court require Afidavits of the person applying to be the Administrator of the estate.

Check your accuracy with your instructor. If you made any errors in spelling or terminology, drill each word for one minute.

5- OR 10-MINUTE TIMINGS

Read the following passages carefully. Set your speed and accuracy goals and then take either a five- or ten-minute timing on each.

TIMING 1

The person responsible for administering an estate is either	12
an Executor appointed under a Will or an Administrator	23
appointed by the court. The duties and responsibilities of	35
an Executor or an Administrator are the same.	44
The primary role of an Executor or Administrator is to act	56
as a fiduciary, which means a person in a position of trust.	68
This person is required to handle the estate in a business-	80
like manner, making prudent investment choices, etc. All	91
actions taken must be in the best interests of the benefi-	103
ciaries or heirs-at-law. If the Executor or Administrator	115

• • • •1• • • •2• • • •3• • • •4• • • •5• • • •6• • • •7• • • •8• • • •9• • • •10• • • •11• • • •12

PARAGRAPH 3

A Royal Commission is normally set up to investigate a single topic; for example, the Sullivan Commission on Education (British Columbia). It is not unusual, however, for a Royal Commission to be established to investigate alleged wrongdoings by government officials; for example, the McDonald Commission, which investigated the RCMP. There is no guarantee that recommendations made by a Royal Commission will be acted on by a government or even that the Commission's report will be made public.

PARAGRAPH 4

Parliamentary committees or sub-committees differ from Royal Commissions in that they are composed of Members of Parliament (federal level) or Members of the Legislative Assembly (provincial level). Another major difference is that the report of a parliamentary committee or sub-committee has to be tabled in the House of Commons (federal) or the Provincial Legislative Assembly (provincial). This means that the public will have access to the committee recommendations.

COMPREHENSION 3

Read the following sentences carefully. Key each sentence once, correcting all errors in fact, terminology, spelling, grammar, and punctuation. Use your dictionary and office handbook.

1. If a Will exists, an administrator should be named in in it.

2. "Dying inestate" means that the diceased did not leave a will.

3. One of the duties of an Executor or Administrator are to prepare a schedule of teh deceaseds assets and libilities.

4. An application must be made to the court for an Executor to adminster an estate

5. A negative Wills search does no necessarily mean that no will exists.

6. Assertain whether or not he wants to act at an executor.

7. The Wills area of law involves the prepration of wills for people who is dead.

8. The legal support staff must not become a crutch for the bereaved family members.

9. The court requires prove of the death of deceased.

PARAGRAPH 5

The Parliament of Canada has two houses: the House of
Commons and the Senate. If the federal government decides
to enact a new law as a result of public pressure or reports
from a special commission or committee, the proposed new law
will be introduced in the House of Commons in the form of a
bill. While bills are normally introduced in the House of
Commons, they also can be introduced in the Senate. Bills
introduced in the House of Commons can be identified because
they have a "C" in front of the bill number; e.g., Bill
C-45. Bills introduced in the Senate have an "S" in front
of the bill number; e.g., Bill S-23.

PARAGRAPH 6

A federal bill must successfully pass three readings in the
House of Commons and be referred to the Senate (or vice
versa) before it can be given royal assent and proclaimed
into law. At the first reading, the bill is introduced in
the House of Commons, but no debate takes place. At the
second reading, the bill is introduced in the House again by
the minister responsible for the topic covered in the bill.
The bill is debated and, if it passes second reading, it is
sent to an appropriate committee for review and amendment.
At the third reading, the bill is brought back into the
House with all of the required committee recommendations and
amendments. If the third reading is acceptable, a vote is

If the deceased did not leave a Will (died intestate) [11]
or if the deceased made a Will but the Executor has [21]
died (predeceased) or does not want to act as an [31]
Executor, then an application has to be made to [40]
the court for an Administrator to be appointed [49]
to administer the Estate. The duties of an [58]
Executor and an Administrator are the same, [67]
except that an Executor is appointed under a [76]
Will and an Administrator is appointed by the Court. [86]

Under most circumstances, if there is a Will in [95]
existence, it must be probated. Probate is the [104]
procedure by which the court checks the validity [114]
of the Will. Although procedures vary from [123]
province to province, most courts require the last [133]
known original Will of the deceased, proof of [142]
death, schedules of the deceased's assets and [151]
liabilities, and Affidavits of the Executor(s). [160]

If no Will can be found, an application to the [169]
court for the appointment of an Administrator [178]
will require proof that an exhaustive Wills [187]
search has been conducted. Such an application [196]
also requires proof of death, schedules of the [205]
deceased's assets and liabilities, and Affidavits [215]
of the person applying to be the Administrator of [225]
the estate — often a family member. [232]

taken by the House and the bill is passed to the Senate, where it is given three readings and a committee review. If the bill passes the Senate, it is sent to the Governor General for his or her signature. This process is called "royal assent." The bill is then known as a "Statute" or an "Act." If the Act contains a proclamation date, then it becomes law on that date. In the absence of a proclamation date, the Act becomes law when royal assent has been received.

3-MINUTE TIMINGS

Read the following passages carefully. Set your speed and accuracy goals and then take a three-minute timing of each.

TIMING 1

Although an Act is proclaimed and in force (meaning | 11
that the courts can enforce the law in the Act), the | 21
law - making process often does not stop at this point. | 32
Many times when making new laws, federal and | 41
provincial governments will merely cover the | 50
barebones of the topic in the proclaimed Act. This | 60
is because government officials often do not have | 70

Soon after the law firm has been approached to handle an | 11
estate matter, the assigned lawyer and appropriate legal | 22
support staff meet with family members to obtain as much | 33
information as possible about the deceased. This infor- | 44
mation will include details of employment, bank accounts, | 55
investments, pensions, life insurance policies, etc. Much | 67
of the information may be sketchy and, therefore, further | 78
investigation will be required. | 84

One of the first things that must be done on an estate file | 96
is to ascertain whether the deceased left a Will. This | 107
involves searching your provincial records to see whether | 118
the deceased recorded the making of his or her Will with | 129
the government authorities. Recording of the making of a | 140
Will is not a requirement in most provinces, so a Wills | 151
search producing a negative result does not necessarily | 162
mean that no Will exists. | 167

If a Will does exist, an Executor should be named in it. | 178
The next step is to find the Executor, interview him or | 189
her, and ascertain whether he or she wants to act as | 199
Executor. Being an Executor is a very time-consuming job, | 211
so many Executors choose to have law firms act on their | 222
behalf. | 223

· · · · 1 · · · · 2 · · · · 3 · · · · 4 · · · · 5 · · · · 6 · · · · 7 · · · · 8 · · · · 9 · · · · 10 · · · · 11 · · · · 12

the expertise or the time to read and understand
lengthy laws. In addition, they know that in the
future they will not have time to consider and
pass minor amendments to the many Acts they
proclaim. Despite this barebones approach, most
Acts have embedded in them a provision (called
an "enabling section") whereby an appropriate
cabinet minister can establish regulations under
the Act. These regulations are usually very
detailed and establish how the Act is to be implemented.

    Regulations have the same force and effect
as the main Act and, for this reason, are often
referred to as "subsidiary legislation."

    Sometimes the work of establishing and
administering regulations under a particular Act
is delegated to a special authorized body called a
"regulatory body." These regulatory bodies often have
the power to order people to appear before them and
explain contraventions of regulations.

TIMING 2 (3 min)

Two other forms of legislative process are the provincial legislative process and the municipal legislative
process. The provincial legislative process is very similar
to the federal process. Bills have two readings, a com-

· · · ·1· · · ·2· · · ·3· · · ·4· · · ·5· · · ·6· · · ·7· · · ·8· · · ·9· · · ·10· · · ·11· · · ·12

3-MINUTE TIMINGS

Read the following passages carefully. Set your speed and accuracy goals and then take a three-minute timing on each.

TIMING 1

While the Wills area of law involves the preparation of	11
Wills for people who are alive, the Estates area of law	22
involves the handling of estates of people who have died.	33
Generally, a law firm is approached by a family member	44
or the Executor named in the Will of the deceased (if a	55
Will has been located) and asked to act on behalf of the	66
Executor or Administrator of the estate.	74
All legal support staff involved in Estate work have to	85
demonstrate tact, diplomacy, and maturity in handling	96
this delicate area of law. When someone has died, the	107
surviving family members are often extremely distressed.	118
It is critical, however, that the legal support staff do	129
not become a crutch for the bereaved.	136
While an Estate lawyer oversees the legal work being done	147
and handles complex estate matters, there are many oppor-	158
tunities for legal support staff to become involved in	169
research work, such as ascertaining the assets and liabili-	181
ties of the deceased. For this reason, Estates can be a	192
very rewarding area of law in which to work.	201

· · · · 1 · · · · 2 · · · · 3 · · · · 4 · · · · 5 · · · · 6 · · · · 7 · · · · 8 · · · · 9 · · · · 10 · · · · 11 · · · · 12

mittee review, and then a third reading. Provincial governments have only one House, so the bill is passed straight
to the Lieutenant-Governor of the province for his or her
signature. The Act comes into force on the proclamation
date. In the absence of a proclamation date, the effective date of the Act will depend on the province's law.
Some provinces use the term "regulation date" instead of
proclamation date but it means the same thing.

As with the federal law-making process, provinces can
enact regulations. Where federal regulations are published
in The Canada Gazette, provincial regulations are published
in the provincial equivalent of The Gazette. In the case of
both federal and provincial regulations, there are some
publishing exemptions.

The law-making process at the municipal level consists
of by-laws, not Acts or regulations. Generally, the by-law
goes through the committee review stage before the three
readings. Another major difference is that the three
readings usually take place at one sitting of Council;
however, there is usually a one-day reconsideration period
between the third reading and the adoption of the by-law.

Certain by-laws, such as those relating to rezoning,
require that a public hearing take place before adoption. A
by-law that will require a municipality to borrow money,
such as for the building of a new municipal sports complex,
would require a public vote (referendum).

. . . . 1 . . . . 2 . . . . 3 . . . . 4 . . . . 5 . . . . 6 . . . . 7 . . . . 8 . . . . 9 . . . .10 . . . .11 12

their discretion, the bills, notes, guarantees or other securities or contracts evidencing such liability and for that purpose, to enter into new bills, notes, guarantees or other securities or contracts for and on behalf of my estate.

CLAUSE 6

1.   I HEREBY REVOKE Paragraph 8.0 of my Last Will and Testament which reads as follows:

> "IN THE EVENT that my said wife shall predecease me, or surviving me, shall die within a period of thirty (30) days after the date of my death, then I APPOINT my said niece, TANIA ADELE COHEN, to be the Guardian of my infant children alive at the time of my decease during their respective minorities."

AND I HEREBY DIRECT that the following be inserted as Paragraph 8.0 of my Last Will and Testament:

> "IN THE EVENT that my said wife shall predecease me, or surviving me, shall die within a period of thirty (30) days after the date of my death, then I APPOINT my said nephew, ALEX KARL BILINSKI, to be the Guardian of my infant children alive at the time of my decease during their respective minorities."

Once a bill has received royal assent, it is known by |12
its title; for example, the Company Act. The bill number |23
is no longer used. The title of an Act indicates its |34
content; for example, the Company Act contains the laws |45
pertaining to companies. |50

When citing the name of an Act, it is important to know |62
whether the "t" of the word "the" needs to be capitalized. |73
The article "the" is not considered as part of the name of |84
any federal Act, so it is not capitalized; e.g., the Divorce |96
Act. The same rule applies to Acts passed by British |107
Columbia, New Brunswick, Nova Scotia, Quebec, the Northwest |119
Territories, and the Yukon. The article "the" is considered |131
part of the name of Acts passed in Alberta, Manitoba, |142
Newfoundland, Ontario, Prince Edward Island, and |151
Saskatchewan, so the "t" is capitalized. |159

At the end of the government session, all Acts that |170
have been passed are assigned a chapter number and published |182
in bound volumes identified by the year. Acts passed by the |194
federal government will be placed in the Statutes of Canada |206
(S.C.). Acts passed by provincial governments are entitled |218
with the provincial name; for example, the Statutes of Nova |230
Scotia (S.N.S.). From time to time, governments consolidate |242
their laws and issue new volumes that are then known as the |254
Revised Statutes of Canada (R.S.C.) or the Revised Statutes |266
of Nova Scotia (R.S.N.S.). Because Acts are organized in |277

. . . .1. . . .2. . . .3. . . .4. . . .5. . . .6. . . .7. . . .8. . . .9. . . .10. . . .11. . . .12

any Codicil hereto, whether such duties or taxes be payable in respect of estates or interest which fall into possession at my death or at any subsequent time; AND I AUTHORIZE my Trustees to prepay or commute any such duty or taxes. This direction shall not apply to any taxes that may be payable by a Purchaser or Transferee in connection with any property transferred to or acquired by such Purchaser or Transferee upon or after my death, pursuant to any agreement with respect to such property.

CLAUSE 4

4.8   As to any investments held by my estate, including any investment in or in connection with any company or corporation, I EMPOWER my Trustees to join in or take any action in connection with such investments or to exercise any rights, powers and privileges which at any time may exist or arise in connection with any such investments to the same extent and as fully as I could if I were alive and the sole owner thereof.

CLAUSE 5

5.6   If, at the time of my death I am liable as endorser, guarantor, surety or otherwise for any company or person or persons, I EMPOWER my Trustees to renew from time to time, in

this way, it is possible to cite Acts so that other people | 289 |
can find them quickly. An example of an Act citation would | 301 |
be: the Company Act, R.S.B.C. 1979, c.59. This means that | 313 |
if you looked at chapter 59 of the Revised Statutes of | 324 |
British Columbia for 1979 you would find the Company Act. | 335 |

If you want to refer someone to a particular section of | 347 |
an Act, you can do this by adding to the citation; for exam- | 359 |
ple, the Company Act, R.S.B.C. 1979, c.59, s.200(2)(a)(ii). | 371 |
In this case, you would be referring to section 200, sub- | 382 |
section (2)(a)(ii). | 386 |

. . . .1. . . .2. . . .3. . . .4. . . .5. . . .6. . . .7. . . .8. . . .9. . . .10. . . .11. . . .12

COMPREHENSION 3

Read the following sentences carefully. Key each sentence once, correcting all errors in fact, terminology, spelling, grammar, and punctuation. Use your dictionary and office handbook.

1. They made recommendation regarding the repeel of the oout-of-date Act.

2. Royal Commissions differ from parliamentary committes in that they are composed of Members of Parliament or Members of the Legislature Assembly.

3. The Parliament of Canada have two houses: the House of of Commons and the Senate.

CLAUSE 2

3.1   To sell, call in and convert into money all my
        assets not consisting of money, except as
        otherwise specifically disposed of by this my
        Will or any Codicil thereto, at such times and
        upon such terms as my Trustees deem advisable,
        with power to postpone the sale or conversion of
        any part of my estate for such length of time as
        they may consider best, AND I HEREBY DECLARE that
        my Trustees may retain any portion of my estate
        in the form in which it may be at my death
        (notwithstanding that it may not be in the form
        of an investment in which Trustees are authorized
        to invest trust funds, and whether or not there
        is a liability attached to any such portion of
        my estate) for such length of time as my said
        Trustees may, in their discretion, deem advisable.

CLAUSE 3

3.2   To pay out of the capital of my estate my just
debts, funeral and testamentary expenses and all succession
duties, inheritance and death taxes, whether imposed by or
pursuant to the laws of this or any other jurisdiction,
including such that may be payable in connection with any
insurance on my life or any gift or benefit given by me
either in my lifetime or by survivorship or by my Will or

4. A federal bill is sent for committee review after first reading in the House.

5. The process of the Governor General signing a provincial bill is called "royal ascent."

6. If theAct contains a proclaimation date, then it becomes law on that date.

7. Regulations are usually very detailed and establish how an Act is to be implemented.

8. Federal regulations are published in The Canadian Gazette.

9. The law-making process at the muncipal level consist of regulations.

10. The article "the" is not considered part of the name of any federal Act.

11. From time to time the federal governments review their laws and issue new volumes called the Revise Statues of Canada (R.S.C).

12. When an Act is declared into force the courts can enforce the law contained in it.

Check your accuracy with your instructor. If you made any errors, drill the words for one minute.

COMPREHENSION 2

Indicate your knowledge of the following terms by using each one in a separate sentence. If you are uncertain of any words, use your dictionary.

attestation clause	execution
revocation	intestate
Codicil	heirs-at-law
beneficiary	issue
residue	probate

PARAGRAPH PRACTICE

Read the following Will and Codicil clauses and then key an accurate copy of each one. If you make any errors, drill each word correctly for one minute.

CLAUSE 1

2.   I APPOINT JACINTH SAMJI to be the Executrix and Trustee of this my Will. Should the said JACINTH SAMJI predecease, refuse, or be unable to act, or continue to act, or requests to be discharged then I APPOINT MARITIME TRUST COMPANY LIMITED to be the Executor in her place. The expression "Trustees" shall mean and include the Executor or Executors and the Trustee or Trustees for the time being hereof whether original, additional, or substituted.

5- OR 10-MINUTE TIMINGS

Read the following passages carefully. Set your speed and accuracy goals and then take either a five- or ten-minute timing for each.

TIMING 1

Provincial legislatures have jurisdiction over the	11
administration of justice within their provinces. This	22
includes the creation and maintenance of the courts.	32
Because each province can create its own court system,	43
the names of the courts vary across Canada. The	53
court systems can be loosely categorized into four	63
areas: lower courts, intermediate courts, superior	73
courts, and appeal courts. Some provinces have	82
courts in each of these categories, while others do not.	93
Most of the lower courts within the	101
provinces are called the "Provincial Courts" and	111
have a series of divisions, such as the criminal	121
division, juvenile division, family division, civil	131
division, traffic division, etc. Others are named	141
for the topic they cover; for example, Small	150
Claims Court.	153
These lower provincial courts hear offences	163
under the Criminal Code (criminal division), offences	174
by young offenders (juvenile division), matters relating	185
to division of property, separation, etc. (family	195

WITNESS WHEREOF in capital letters; and (k) an attestation

clause wherein the two witnesses to the Will attest that

they were present when the Testator/Testatrix signed the

Will and that they saw him or her sign it.

····1····2····3····4····5····6····7····8····9····10····11····12

TIMING 4

Executing a Will

One of the duties of legal support personnel is to act
as a witness to the execution (signing) of a Will.
You should take this duty seriously. You are required
to watch the Testator or Testatrix sign the Will and
initial beside the last word on each page, except the
last page. Once you have witnessed the signing, you
sign as a witness on the last page of the Will. You
fill in your address and occupation and then initial
each page beside the Testator's/Testatrix's initials.
The second witness then goes through the same
process. It is critical that all parties watch all
other parties sign and witness the document.

If a small error is detected at the time of signing
a Will, the error can be changed in ink and
initialled by all parties; however, with the speed
of word processing, most lawyers prefer to have
the error corrected properly and a new page or
pages prepared. If a Testator decides to change a
Will after it has been signed, the above procedure
cannot be used: a Codicil must be prepared instead.

3
14
24
35
45
56
66
76
86
97
106
116
125

135
144
154
163
172
182
192
202

division), claims for payment of small sums of money, usually under $5,000 (small claims division, civil division), and traffic offences (traffic division).

The intermediate or second level of courts in the provinces are usually called either "County Court" or "District Court." These courts usually hear civil cases between certain dollar figures, such as between $5,000 and $50,000; conduct criminal trials; and hear appeals from the criminal, family, and small claims divisions of the lower courts. County Court Judges hear cases alone or with a jury.

The superior or third level of courts in the provinces are usually called either the "Supreme Court" of the province (e.g., the Supreme Court of British Columbia); the Court of Queen's Bench; the Superior Court; or the Supreme Court, Trial Division. These are the highest trial courts in the provinces and usually hear serious criminal cases, including those that are listed in the Criminal Code as having to be tried at the superior court level. Most superior court criminal trials are heard by a Judge and jury. The superior court also hears defended (contested) divorce cases; civil cases involving amounts of, for example, more than $50,000; and some appeal cases from the first level of courts.

graph, should be numbered for identification purposes. For
example, if a Testator/Testatrix wants to change the wording
of one clause in his or her Will at a later date, the
paragraph can be identified by number when the Codicil is
prepared.

179
191
202
213
215

· · · ·1· · · ·2· · · ·3· · · ·4· · · ·5· · · ·6· · · ·7· · · ·8· · · ·9· · · ·10· · · ·11· · · ·12

TIMING 3

Contents of a Will

4

The contents, or provisions, of a standard Will include
the following: (a) an introductory paragraph naming the
Testator/Testatrix; (b) a revocation clause revoking (can-
celling) all previously made Wills; (c) a clause giving
instructions regarding funeral arrangements; (d) a clause
appointing one or more Executors and Trustees; (e) a series
of clauses instructing the Executor(s) and Trustee(s) to
pay all debts, funeral, and administrative expenses; (f) a
series of clauses instructing the Executor(s) and Trustee(s)
to distribute gifts of property and cash to named beneficiaries, including children under the age of majority; (g)
a series of clauses regarding investments the Trustee is
empowered to make; (h) a clause outlining how the residue
(the remainder) of the estate of the deceased is to be
distributed once all debts have been paid and all beneficiaries, including children under the age of majority;
(g) a series of clauses regarding investments the Trustee is
testimonium clause usually beginning with the words IN

15
26
38
49
60
72
83
95
107
118
129
141
152
163
174
185
196
207

· · · ·1· · · ·2· · · ·3· · · ·4· · · ·5· · · ·6· · · ·7· · · ·8· · · ·9· · · ·10· · · ·11· · · ·12

The appellate or fourth level of courts in the provinces are usually called either the "Court of Appeal" or the "Supreme Court, Appeal Division." These are the highest courts in the provinces and hear appeals from the Trials Division of the Supreme Court and appeals relating to both criminal and civil cases from the lower courts. Appeal courts have an odd number of Judges (usually three or five) as opposed to one Judge in any of the other courts.

452
461
470
479
489
495
504
513
522
532

TIMING 2 (5 or 10 min)

Other courts in the Canadian court system include the Federal Court of Canada, the Supreme Court of Canada, and the Citizenship Court. There are also some special courts, such as the Surrogate Court and the Court of Revision.

The Federal Court of Canada, located in Ottawa, was established in 1970 by the Federal Court Act, R.S.C. 1970, c.10 (2d Supp.). It hears disputes between individuals, groups, or corporations and the federal government; appeals from federal tribunals and boards; and cases relating to copyright, patents, trademarks, and admiralty matters.

The Federal Court has two divisions: the Trial Division and the Appeals Division. Disputes are heard in the Trial Division first and then, if the parties want to appeal, they do so to the Appeals Division. If the parties

12
23
35
46
57
69
80
92
103
114
124
135
146
158

. . . . 1 . . . . 2 . . . . 3 . . . . 4 . . . . 5 . . . 6 . . . . 7 . . . 8 . . . 9 . . . . 10 . . . . 11 12

to dictate long and complicated legal material. Another
advantage is that the wording of the precedent clauses is
usually accurate and proven. This means that, over the
years, these clauses have not proved to be contentious--
Wills have not been contested in court as a result of
ambiguous or incorrect wording.

130
141
152
163
174
180

TIMING 2

Format of a Will

Wills are usually prepared on Wills paper, which is of good
quality and has red vertical lines denoting the margins.

The first page of a Will should have a 5-cm (2-inch) top
margin. Subsequent pages should have a margin of approximately 4 cm (1 1/2 inches). The bottom margin of each page
should be 2.5 cm (1 inch) in depth. The side margins are
delineated by the vertical red lines. You should set your
margins to within a couple of spaces of each of the red
lines. Under no circumstances should any words extend
beyond the red lines.

The body of the Will should be double-spaced, with triple
spacing between paragraphs. The attestation clause at the
end of the Will is single-spaced.

Because Wills are top-bound, page numbers should be at the
bottom of each page.

All Wills clauses, with the exception of the opening para-

3
15
26
37
49
61
72
84
95
106
110
121
133
140
152
156
167

want to appeal again, they can appeal to the Supreme Court of Canada.

The Supreme Court of Canada, which is also located in Ottawa, is the final court of appeal in Canada for both criminal and civil cases. Its jurisdiction is governed by the Supreme Court Act, R.S.C. 1970, c.S-19. It differs from other courts in that it can choose the cases it will hear; therefore, parties wanting to appeal their cases to the Supreme Court of Canada must first make an application. The Court will not take on frivolous cases: it concentrates on those that are of national importance or involve issues of law.

The Supreme Court of Canada is a very formal court. Both the Judges and the lawyers are specially gowned. As with the provincial appeal courts, the Supreme Court of Canada has an odd number of Judges who review the written record of the original court and the subsequent appeal courts and hear presentations from the lawyers for both parties in the dispute. Usually there are no other people present in the courtroom because the facts of the case have already been established in the lower courts. The job of the Supreme Court (as with any appeal court) is to examine the points of law.

The Supreme Court of Canada also hears disputes between the provinces or between a province and the federal government. It also gives the federal government advice on constitutional matters.

. . . . 1 . . . . 2 . . . . 3 . . . . 4 . . . . 5 . . . . 6 . . . . 7 . . . . 8 . . . . 9 . . . . 10 . . . . 11 12

11. An Executor or Administrator must account to the beneficiaries or heirs-at-law for all of the assets of the deceased, all monies received, and all assets and monies disbursed and/or distributed.

12. If a beneficiary or heir-at-law is not satisfied with the Executor's or Administrator's accounts, he or she may apply to the Court for a passing of accounts.

2-MINUTE TIMINGS

Read the following passages carefully. Set your speed and accuracy goals. Take two-minute timings on each passage.

TIMING 1

When a client approaches a law firm to have a Will prepared, | 12

the lawyer notes the client's wishes and then decides on the | 24

appropriate wording for the Will. Today, most law firms | 35

keep standard precedent Wills clauses on their computer | 46

systems so that a lawyer need only give instructions to the | 58

legal support staff as to which clauses to use in preparing | 70

the Will. If the Will is complicated, the lawyer may use | 81

a combination of standard precedent clauses and tailor-made | 93

clauses. | 95

The major advantages of using standard Wills clauses is that | 107

time and money can be saved because the lawyer does not have | 119

· · · ·1· · · ·2· · · ·3· · · ·4· · · ·5· · · ·6· · · ·7· · · ·8· · · ·9· · · ·10· · · ·11· · · ·12

The Citizenship Court is a specialized federal court | 443
that is convened to grant Canadian citizenship to immi- | 454
grants. It is a ceremonial court. | 461

Two special courts are the Surrogate Court and the | 472
Court of Revision. The Surrogate Court probates (authenti- | 484
cates) Wills of people who have died and handles the admin- | 496
istration of the estates of people who have died without | 507
leaving Wills. The Court of Revision is a temporary court | 519
that is convened at certain times of the year, specifically | 531
after property tax assessments have been mailed to home- | 542
owners. The function of this Court is to hear homeowners' | 554
disputes of their property tax assessments. | 563

. . . .1. . . .2. . . .3. . . .4. . . .5. . . .6. . . .7. . . .8. . . .9. . . .10. . . .11. . . .12

TIMING 3 (5 or 10 min)

WHO'S WHO | 2

Judges: A provincial lower court Judge, sometimes called a | 14
"magistrate," is usually appointed and paid by the provin- | 26
cial government. County, Supreme, and Appeal Court Judges | 38
are usually appointed and paid by the federal government. | 49
The function of a Judge varies, depending on whether he or | 61
she is hearing a case alone or with a jury. If a Judge is | 73
hearing a case alone, he or she will have to ascertain the | 85
facts, look at the law (either statute law or case law or | 96
a combination of both), and make a decision, called a | 106

. . . .1. . . .2. . . .3. . . .4. . . .5. . . .6. . . .7. . . .8. . . .9. . . .10. . . .11. . . .12

2. When two or more people are named in a Will as Executors, they are referred to as "Co-Executors."

3. The term "intestate" means dying without having made a Will.

4. "Issue" is the term used to refer to all lawful, lineal descendants, such as children, grand-children, and great-grandchildren.

5. A Codicil is attached to a Will and serves to either change or add clauses to the Will.

6. Probate is the court procedure whereby a Will is proved to be the Last Will and Testament of the deceased.

7. If a person dies intestate (without having made a Will) or testate (but the Executor does not want to act), then the Court must appoint an Administrator to be responsible for the administration of the estate.

8. The duties of an Executor and an Administrator are the same.

9. One of the duties of an Executor or Administrator is to ascertain the assets and liabilities of the deceased.

10. At common law, Executors and Administrators are not entitled to charge for administering an estate; however, each province has a statute allowing Executors and Administrators to charge fees.

WILLS AND ESTATES

"judgment." If the Judge is hearing a case with a jury, then the job of the Judge is to guide the jury.

Court Clerks: A court clerk assists a Judge by looking after the court files and documents, calling the case in court, and swearing in witnesses.

Court Reporters/Recorders: A court reporter/recorder records the court proceedings verbatim (word for word).

Sheriffs: A sheriff handles court security and looks after the accused, the witnesses, and juries. In some provinces, sheriffs are responsible for serving legal documents.

Lawyers: A lawyer is a person who has studied at law school, articled in a law firm or law-related organization, and been accepted into the legal profession (called to the bar). Because a lawyer in Canada is both a barrister and solicitor, he or she can represent clients in court or do non-court work such as Wills and estates, conveyancing, corporate law, etc. A lawyer is a fiduciary, which means that he or she holds a position of trust.

Notaries: A notary public is a person who is authorized to take Affidavits; administer oaths; and execute, certify, and authenticate legal documents. A notary public is NOT a lawyer; however, a lawyer can be a notary public.

Law Societies: Each province has a law society, which consists of "benchers"--lawyers who are elected or appointed

is a member of the Canadian Armed Forces on active duty.

You should check your provincial Wills Act.

····1····2····3····4····5····6····7····8····9····10····11····12

Did you achieve your speed and accuracy goals on at least one of the timings? If not, repeat the timings.

COMPREHENSION 1

Key the following sentences once, filling in each blank with the appropriate legal term or phrase.

1. --- is the plural term for female Executors.

2. A legal document amending a Will is called a ---.

3. If a --- or spouse of a --- witnesses a Will, the gift is ---.

4. A man who makes a Will is called a --- . A woman who makes a Will is called a ---.

5. A handwritten Will that is not witnessed is called a --- Will.

6. Your provincial --- stipulates the restrictions on who can make a Will.

Check your answers with your instructor.

SENTENCE PRACTICE

Read the following sentences carefully. Key each sentence once. Concentrate on accuracy and rhythmic keying.

1. I revoke all former Wills and testamentary dispositions heretofore made by me.

to oversee the activities of other lawyers and law firms. | 378

Most law societies have a few lay benchers but are generally | 390

considered to be self-governing bodies serving two masters: | 402

the public and the lawyers. They perform many functions: | 413

they regulate the profession (call lawyers to the bar, | 424

handle complaints from the public against lawyers, disci- | 435

pline lawyers, disbar lawyers), provide advisory services to | 447

lawyers, and offer skills training to lawyers and legal | 458

support staff. Lawyers are levied annual fees and errors- | 469

and-omissions insurance premiums by their law societies. | 480

Official Guardians: Provinces have official guardians who | 492

are responsible for representing minors (people who are not | 504

yet of the age of majority). In some provinces the Public | 516

Trustee performs this function. | 522

Public Trustees: Public Trustees are responsible for | 532

representing minors and people who are mentally incompetent. | 544

····1····2····3····4····5····6····7····8····9····10····11····12

PRODUCTION EXERCISES

EXERCISE 1

Taking information contained in Timing 3 on page 17, prepare a table that shows the names of the provinces in alphabetical order and whether the word "the" is considered to be part of the names of their Acts. Time yourself to see how quickly you can complete this work. Remember that accuracy is extremely important.

TIMING 3

For a Will to be legally valid, it must be in writing and | 11

signed on the last page by the Testator/Testatrix in the | 22

presence of two witnesses. The Testator/Testatrix and | 33

witnesses should initial beside the last word on each page | 45

so that no words can be added following signing. A hand- | 56

written Will that is not witnessed is called a "holographic | 68

Will." Such Wills are not generally valid. | 77

` . . . .1. . . .2. . . .3. . . .4. . . .5. . . .6. . . .7. . . .8. . . .9. . . .10. . . .11. . . .12`

TIMING 4

Witnesses to a Will must be of legal age and not be | 10

a beneficiary or the spouse of a beneficiary named | 20

in the Will. If a beneficiary or spouse of a beneficiary | 31

witnesses a Will, the Will remains valid but the gift | 42

to the witness or his or her spouse is void. The two | 53

witnesses must both be present at the same time | 62

and must watch the Testator/Testatrix sign. | 71

TIMING 5

Your provincial Wills Act stipulates the restrictions on who | 12

can make a Will. Generally speaking, an individual must | 23

be of the age of majority and be of sound mind, memory, | 34

and understanding. Usually an individual under the age of | 46

majority may make a Will if he or she is married, has been | 58

married, is a seaman or mariner at sea or on a voyage, or | 69

` . . . .1. . . .2. . . .3. . . .4. . . .5. . . .6. . . .7. . . .8. . . .9. . . .10. . . .11. . . .12`

Read the following material, watching for errors. Set yourself a production time limit and then key the material quickly and accurately. Box the end-product.

LEGAL ETHICS

Lawyers must discharge their duties to clients, the courts, the public, and members of the legal profession with courtesy, good faith, and integrity.

Lawyers and legal support staff should help to maintain the the integrity of the profession.

Lawyers should be open and honest when advicing clients.

Lawyers and legal support staff should provide competant, quality service.

Lawyers should not withdraw their services to clients except for good cause and with appropriate notice.

Lawyers and legal support staff should hold in strict confidence all information that they acquire concerning the business and affairs of clients. They must not divulge any such information unless required by law or unless their clients give them permission to do so.

Lawyers should not advise or represent both slides of a dispute.

1-MINUTE TIMINGS

Read the following paragraphs carefully. Set your speed and accuracy goals. Take one-minute timings on each paragraph.

TIMING 1

```
A Will is a written legal document that expresses the wishes     12
of the person making the Will as far as the disposition of       24
his or her property upon death.  If a man makes and executes     36
(signs) a Will, he is called the "Testator."  If a woman         47
makes and executes a Will she is called the "Testatrix."  A      59
legal document amending a Last Will and Testament is called      71
a Codicil.                                                       73
```
. . . . 1 . . . . 2 . . . . 3 . . . . 4 . . . . 5 . . . . 6 . . . . 7 . . . . 8 . . . . 9 . . . .10. . . .11. . . .12

TIMING 2

```
A man named in a Will to carry out the wishes of the            11
Testator or Testatrix upon death, is called the "Executor."      23
The female term is "Executrix."  If there is more than one       35
male Executor, the term "Executors" is used.  If there is        46
more than one female Executrix, the term "Executrices" is        57
used.  Many lawyers use the term "Executor(s)" instead of        68
"Executrix(ces)."                                                71
```
. . . . 1 . . . . 2 . . . . 3 . . . . 4 . . . . 5 . . . . 6 . . . . 7 . . . . 8 . . . . 9 . . . .10. . . .11. . . .12

Lawyers and legal support staff should obey all relevant laws regarding the preservation and safekeeping of client's property.

Lawyers should not stipulate, charge, or accept a fees that is not fully disclosed, fair, and reasonable. Client trust funds must not be used to pay legal fees without the permission of the client.

Lawyers should encourage public respect for, and try to improve the administration of, justice.

Lawyers should try to prevent any unauthorized practice of of law.

Adapted from The Canadian Bar Association, *Code of Professional Conduct*.

EXERCISE 3

Read the following extracts from a legal office handbook, watching for errors. Set yourself a production time limit and then key the material quickly and accurately.

Statute Abbreviations

The "R." in the abbreviation stands for "Statute." The remaining letters in the abreviation refer to the country or province name.

Examples:

Statutes of Canada	S.C.
Statutes of Alberta	A.S.

WORD PRACTICE

Key one line of each of the following words. Concentrate on accuracy and rhythmic keying.

Will	nominate
Codicil	devise
execution	bequeath
revocation	testate
issue	intestate
Testator	deceased
Executor	heirs
Trustee	probate
beneficiary	renunciation
escheat	Testatrix

PHRASE PRACTICE

Key each of the following phrases six times. Concentrate on accuracy. Say each phrase to yourself as you key it. Remember to key rhythmically.

Last Will and Testament
who died intestate
any issue her surviving
renunciation of probate
I hereby revoke

assets of the deceased
shall predecease me
in the said estate
Executor and Trustee
any Codicil thereto

Statutes of British Columbia	S.B.C.
Statutes of Manitoba	S.M.
Statutes of New Brunswick	S.N.B.

Revised Statute Abbreviations

The "R.S." at the beginning of the abbreviation stands for "Revised Statues." The remainder of the abbreviation relates to to the province name.

Examples:

Revised Statutes of Alberta	R.S.A.
Revised Statutes of British Columbia	R.S.B.C.
Revised Statutes of Manitoba	R.S.S.
Revised Statutes of New Brunswick	R.S.N.B.

Case Law Report Abbreviations

The follow is a list of some of teh most commonly used case law report abbreviations. You will find others listed in Banks, M.A. Using a Law Library: A Guide for Students and Lawyers in the Common Law Provinces of Canada. 4th ed. Toronto: The Carswell Company Limited, 1985.

All E.R.	All England Law Reports, 1936-
App. Cas.	Law Reports, Apeal Cases, 1875-1890
C.C.C.	Canadian Criminal Cases, 1893-1962
C.C.C.(3d)	Canadian Criminal Cases (Third Series), 1983-
C.R.(3d)	Criminal Reports (Third Series), 1978-
D.L.R.	Dominion Law Reports, 1912-1922

Wills
and Estates

O.L.R.	Ontario Law Reports, 1901-1931
O.W.N.	Ontario Weekley Notes, 1909-1932
[ ] Que.C.A.	Quebec Official Reports (Court of Appeal), 1970-
R.F.L.	Reports of Family Law, 1971-1977
S.C.R.	Reports of teh Supeme Court of Canada, 1876-1922
[ ] W.L.R.	Weekly Law Reports, 1953
W.L.R.	Western Law Reporter, 1905-1916

Recognizing that in handling this conveyance you will be incuring disbursements and giving your undertaking to other persons/corporations, we understand and agree that this Authority to Pay is irrevokable unless and to the extent that you may consent otherwise.

We confirm that some of the figures set out above have been received by you from third parties and that the actual figures may vary.

Dated at (your city), (your province), this day of   , 19--.

_____   _____
ERIC JURILOFF   SONYA JURILOFF

Adapted from Guide to Conveyancing, 3-137.

Working in a Law Firm

Read the following Authority to Pay, watching for errors. Set yourself a production time limit and then key the document quickly and accurately in full block style.

AUTHORITY TO PAY

To: OKAZAKI, McGEE & CO., Barrister and Solicitor, 4908
        49th Street, Yellowknife, Yukon Territory X1A 2N7

Re: Purchase of 49877 Kipp Avenue, Chilliwack, B.C.
        Legal description: PID# 002-456-987, Lot 12 of D.L.
        678, Group 6, Plan 75962, N.W.D.
        Completion date: March 2, 19--
        Vendor: JOEL TOEWS

This is your irrevokable authority to recieve and disburse the purchase proceeds of the above property as follows:

IN

Funds ot be provided by
ERIC AND SONYA JURILOFF $94,382.18

                          TOTAL FUNDS IN: $94,382.18

OUT

To JOEL TOEWS $76,371.58

To WADDELL & CO. (Realtor)   12,780.00

To OKAZAKI, McGEE & CO. - Legal feas   950.00

To OKAZAKI, McGEE & CO. - Disbursements   4,280.60

                         TOTAL FUNDS OUT: $94,332.18

WORD PRACTICE

Key one line of each of the following words. Concentrate on accuracy and rhythmic keying.

lawyer	secretary
partner	support
associate	advice
articling	ethics
administrator	trust
assistant	account
paralegal	fees
clerks	retainer
law	disbursements
firm	dockets

PHRASE PRACTICE

Key each of the following phrases six times. Concentrate on accuracy. Say each phrase to yourself as you key it. Remember to key rhythmically.

partners of the law firm
managing partner and office administrator
junior lawyers and associates
legal assistants, paralegals, and law clerks
legal secretaries and legal support staff
legal advice
legal ethics
fees and disbursements
trust account
articling students

satisfactory pre- and post-registration index searches showing the Title as contemplated by the Contract of Purchase and Sale, to pay to your firm in trust the balance due to the Vendor on completion as set out in the Vendors' Statement of Adjustments and to pay the balance of real estate commission.

Yours truly,
MISHRA, DENT & ARMITSTEAD

Per:
Sharin Mishra
SM/
Encs.

Adapted from *Guide to Conveyancing*, 3-187.

1-MINUTE TIMINGS

Read the following paragraphs carefully. Set your speed and accuracy goals. Take one-minute timings on each paragraph.

TIMING 1

Law firms are partnerships in which usually all of the	11
partners are lawyers. Because few lawyers are experienced	23
in office management, most law firms employ an office	33
manager or administrator to oversee the day-to-day running	44
of the law firm. Sometimes a senior partner, often known as	56
the "managing partner," takes on the responsibilities of	67
running the law firm.	71

. . . . 1 . . . . 2 . . . . 3 . . . . 4 . . . . 5 . . . . 6 . . . . 7 . . . . 8 . . . . 9 . . . . 10 . . . . 11 12

TIMING 2

To become a lawyer, it is usually necessary to have a uni-	11
versity degree, go to law school for approximately three	22
years, and then article in a law firm for a one-year period.	34
During that one-year period, student lawyers have an oppor-	46
tunity to see how a law firm and the law really function.	57
If the student performs well, he or she might be hired by	68
the law firm on a permanent basis at the end of the	78
articling period.	81

. . . . 1 . . . . 2 . . . . 3 . . . . 4 . . . . 5 . . . . 6 . . . . 7 . . . . 8 . . . . 9 . . . . 10 . . . . 11 12

Read the following form letter of undertaking, watching for errors. Set yourself a production time limit and then key the letter quickly and accurately. Transpose paragraphs one and two and number the enclosures in the body of the letter.

Dear   :

Re: Vendor:
       Purchaser:
       Property:
       Completion date:
       File No:

Enclosed are the following documents, in duplicate, for execution by your client:

Freehold Transfer ("the Transferor").
Vendor's Statement of Ajustments.
Vendor's Statutary Declaration re: Section 116 of the Income Tax Act.

We are solicitors for   , Purchaser of the above property, and understand that you act on behalf of the Vendor.

Upon providing us with the executed Vendor's Statement of Adjustment, executed Vendor's Statutary Declaration, and an executed, registerable Transfer, we undertake not to make use of the Transfer in any way until we have in our generalaccount the balance of $ from the Purchaser. Further, we undertake that upon receipt of

TIMING 3

Law firms often have lawyers on staff who specialize in   11
attracting clients to the law firm. You could compare them   23
with the sales force of a company. Until quite recently,   34
lawyers in Canada were not allowed to advertise, which   45
meant that lawyers had to rely on attracting clients by word   57
of mouth and by reputation. Even now, some Law Societies do   69
not permit advertising. In the 1990s, law firms are being   81
forced to be much more competitive than they used to be, so   93
marketing is becoming an issue in many firms.   102

. . . .1. . . .2. . . .3. . . .4. . . .5. . . .6. . . .7. . . .8. . . .9. . . .10. . . .11. . . .12

TIMING 4

When articling students are called to the bar they   10
become lawyers and are permitted to practise law   20
in their province. They are usually classified as   30
junior lawyers or associates at this stage. In   39
larger law firms they usually work under the   48
guidance of a senior lawyer, who may be a   56
partner. Lawyers in Canada are both barristers   65
and solicitors, so their work may or may not   74
involve court appearances.   79

- the gross commision payable, being the total commission due before any other items are taken into consideration;
- the method by which the gross commision is is calculated;
- the amount of deposit held;
- either, (a) the net commision due (where the deposit was less than the gross commision), or (b) the net amount held in excess of the commision (where the deposit was more than the gross commission).

Your truly,

SKIRA, WIEST & CO.

Per:

Harold Wiest

NW/

Adapted from *Guide to Conveyancing*, 4-116.

Most law firms have a ratio of two or more legal support | 11
staff members to each partner. Legal support staff includes | 23
law clerks/paralegals/legal assistants, legal secretaries, | 34
librarians, research assistants, receptionists, switchboard | 46
operators, and mailroom, filing, central services (infor- | 57
mation processing), and accounting personnel. The only way | 69
that law firms receive money is by billing clients; it is of | 81
prime importance, therefore, that all legal office person- | 93
nel provide quality service. | 99

. . . .1. . . .2. . . .3. . . .4. . . .5. . . .6. . . .7. . . .8. . . .9. . . .10. . . .11. . . .12

Did you achieve your speed and accuracy goals on at least one of the timings? If not, repeat the timings.

COMPREHENSION 1

Key the following sentences once, filling in each blank with the appropriate legal term or phrase.

1. Law firms are _partnerships_ --- in which all of the _partners_ --- are lawyers.

2. Sometimes a senior partner, often known as the _managing_ ---, takes on the responsibility of running the law firm.

3. A junior lawyer or _associates_ --- usually works under the guidance of a senior lawyer.

a claim against the property and will probably be filing a Lis Pendens shortly. "Caveat emptor" means "let the buyer beware."

If you are reviewing the Title to a piece of property and you notice either of the last four above charges (a Builder's Lien, a Judgment, a Lis Pendens, or a Caveat) registered against the Title to the property, you should be immediately alerted to the fact that something is seriously wrong and that perhaps the sale or purchase of the property is in jeopardy.

648

658

662

673

683

693

704

714

724

734

PRODUCTION EXERCISES

EXERCISE 1

Read the following form letter requesting real estate information, watching for errors. Set yourself a production time limit and then key the letter quickly and accurately in full block style, single-spaced.

Dear Sirs:

Re: Purchaser:
        Vendor:
        Conpletion date:
        Address of property

We are solicitors for   , Vendor of the above property. Accordingly, we would ask that you provide us with a copy of the Listing contract, together with written confirmation of the following information:

4. When articling students are called to the _bar_
   they become lawyers.
5. Lawyers in Canada are both _barristers_ and _solicitors_, which
   means that they may or may not do court work.
6. The only way that law firms receive money is by
   billing _clients_.

Check your answers with your instructor.

Read the following sentences carefully. Key each sentence once.
Concentrate on accuracy and rhythmic keying.

1. The function of a law firm is to provide legal
   advice to clients.
2. Lawyers, and some legal support personnel, are
   required to keep track of the time they spend
   working for each client.
3. Law firms usually use computerized dockets or
   time cards to keep track of the number of hours
   worked on a particular client file.
4. When a client seeks legal advice, a lawyer is
   required to advise the client of the approximate
   cost of the services being offered.
5. A Retainer Agreement is a written Agreement
   between the law firm and the client that
   stipulates the work to be done, the cost of the

Restrictive Covenant: A Restrictive Covenant restricts what can be done on or to a property. For example, a Restrictive Covenant could disallow mobile homes on the property or only allow certain types of exterior finishes to be added to the buildings.

Statutory Building Scheme: A Statutory Building Scheme is usually placed by the land developer on all the lots in a subdivision to ensure that a particular standard is maintained. For example, a Statutory Building Scheme could stipulate the minimum square footage of the homes being built.

Builder's Lien: A Builder's Lien indicates that someone has done work on the property but has not been paid for it. An example might be if the Vendor had a new roof installed but had not paid the roofing contractor. The contractor would place a Lien against the Vendor's property so that if the Vendor tried to sell the property, the Lien would have to be paid off. A Lien against the Vendor's property is usually a signal to the Purchaser's lawyer that all is not well.

Judgment: A Judgment against the property indicates that the Vendor owes someone money.

Lis Pendens: Lis Pendens is Latin for "litigation pending." It means the Vendor is being sued.

Caveat: "Caveat" is the Latin for "let him beware." This is a caution that someone is intending to make

service, and the amount of the retainer to be given to the law firm.

6. A retainer is an up-front deposit against charges for work the law firm will do.

7. One of the purposes of a retainer is to ensure that the client is really serious about hiring the law firm to represent him or her.

8. Lawyers' charges are known as "fees."

9. Law firms also charge clients for disbursements: sums of money that the law firm pays out on behalf of the client.

10. Some examples of disbursements are long distance telephone calls, fax and telex charges, courier charges, and court filing fees.

11. Law firms usually maintain two types of accounts: general/firm accounts and trust accounts.

12. Trust accounts are used to hold clients' money; therefore, a lawyer must not use this money for his or her own use.

2-MINUTE TIMINGS

Read the following paragraphs carefully. Set your speed and accuracy goals. Take two-minute timings on each paragraph.

is a burden on the land. For example, the Vendor's Mortgage is a charge because the mortgage loan is secured with the property as collateral. This means that when the Vendor originally bought the property, he or she applied for a mortgage. The mortgage monies would have been provided but the Mortgagee would have made sure that some sort of claim was registered against the Vendor's property, in the event that the Vendor ever defaulted on the mortgage payments. This means that the Mortgagee had a claim, or charge, against the property. The Mortgage appears on the Title until it has been paid in full and a Discharge of Mortgage has been filed against the Title.

Besides a Mortgage, the following charges may appear on a title search:

Easement: An Easement is a section of the property that may be used by other parties. A common example of an Easement is the situation in which a neighbour has a driveway (perhaps to access a garage) across the subject property. An Easement usually stays on the property forever.

Right-of-Way: A Right-of-Way is a section of a property that is set aside for access by telephone and power authority personnel. Like an Easement, a Right-of-Way usually remains on the property indefinitely.

TIMING 1

Because law firms have only one source of income--clients-- `12`
they must provide fast, efficient, quality service to remain `24`
in business. For this reason, law firms are very careful `35`
about the personnel they hire. Law firms look for candi- `46`
dates who are mature in attitude, polite, well groomed, `57`
punctual, poised, tactful, discreet, dependable, and orga- `69`
nized. In addition, a candidate must have a pleasant `80`
disposition, be able to produce work quickly and accurately, `92`
and have the ability to follow instructions precisely. All `104`
legal secretaries and legal assistants/paralegals/law clerks `116`
must be familiar with a wide range of computer software `127`
and hardware. They must know the quickest and easiest way `139`
to produce top-quality legal documentation. A sound knowl- `151`
edge of legal office procedures as well as a general back- `163`
ground knowledge of law is essential in these positions. `174`

. . . . 1 . . . . 2 . . . . 3 . . . . 4 . . . . 5 . . . . 6 . . . . 7 . . . . 8 . . . . 9 . . . . 10 . . . . 11 12

TIMING 2

The role of a paralegal/legal assistant/law clerk is some- `11`
what difficult to define, because the job title means dif- `22`
ferent things in different law firms and in different `32`
provinces. For example, in some law firms, paralegals are `44`
senior legal secretaries while in others they are lawyers `55`
who have qualified in another province and are applying for `67`

. . . . 1 . . . . 2 . . . . 3 . . . . 4 . . . . 5 . . . . 6 . . . . 7 . . . . 8 . . . . 9 . . . . 10 . . . . 11 12

On the closing date, the Purchaser's lawyer arranges for | 664
the transfer documents to be registered in the Land Title | 675
Office and for the Vendor to be paid the sale proceeds. | 686

Because the Purchaser's lawyer handles the majority of the | 698
conveyancing documentation and financial transactions, the | 710
Purchaser has to pay the legal fees. The Vendor is respon- | 722
sible for paying the real estate commission and the legal | 733
fees incurred in discharging the Vendor's existing Mortgage. | 745

· · · ·1· · · ·2· · · ·3· · · ·4· · · ·5· · · ·6· · · ·7· · · ·8· · · ·9· · · ·10· · · ·11· · · ·12

TIMING 3 (5 or 10 min)

One of the Purchaser's lawyer's most important tasks is to | 12
conduct a title search. This means that a search of the | 23
property title is conducted in the Land Title Office that | 34
covers the area where the property is to be purchased. | 45
With the computerization of many Land Title Offices, a | 56
search of any property in your province will soon be | 66
able to be conducted from any Land Title Office or | 76
from any computer linked to any Land Title Office. | 86

One of the primary purposes of a title search is to | 96
ensure that the Vendor is the registered owner of the | 107
property. Another purpose is to check to see what | 117
charges are registered against the property. A charge | 128
(sometimes called an "encumbrance," "lien," or "claim") | 139

admission to the bar in the province in which they are 78

working. In certain provinces, independent paralegal ser- 90

vice companies have been established. There is a consider- 102

able difference in the work that these people with the same 114

title might be doing. While some provinces have specialized 126

courses for law clerks and paralegals, others do not. The 138

work of personnel with these job descriptions can include 149

performing senior legal secretarial functions, assisting law- 161

yers in preparing for trial, attending with the lawyer in 172

the courtroom, interviewing witnesses, drafting legal docu- 184

mentation, maintaining contact with clients, etc. One thing 196

is certain, ONLY lawyers can give legal advice. 205

. . . . 1 . . . . 2 . . . . 3 . . . . 4 . . . . 5 . . . . 6 . . . . 7 . . . . 8 . . . . 9 . . . . 10 . . . . 11 12

TIMING 3

Law firms, especially large ones, can offer services 11

in a wide variety of areas, such as banking, bankruptcy, 22

engineering, insurance, immigration, shipping, aviation, 33

land claims, real estate, taxation, wills and estates, 44

securities, personal injury, medical malpractice, criminal 56

law, family matters (divorce, separation, child custody, 67

access, maintenance, adoption, young offenders), corporate 79

law, trademarks, patents, copyright, workers' compensation, 91

international law, administrative law, constitutional 101

law, etc. 103

. . . . 1 . . . . 2 . . . . 3 . . . . 4 . . . . 5 . . . . 6 . . . . 7 . . . . 8 . . . . 9 . . . . 10 . . . . 11 12

Vendor will be credited with the portion of the property taxes from August 31 to December 31 and the Purchaser will be debited with the same amount. In this way, the Vendor is not paying for property taxes when the property does not belong to him or her. Statements of Adjustments are quite complicated financial statements and should always be double-checked by an experienced conveyancer, a lawyer, or both.

The Purchaser's lawyer sends the Transfer document, together with copies of the Vendor's Statement of Adjustments and a letter of undertaking to the Vendor's lawyer and requests that the Vendor sign these documents. The letter of undertaking indicates that the Purchaser's lawyer will not register the Transfer document (signed by the Vendor) in the Land Title Office until there is sufficient money in the law firm's trust account to cover the transaction.

Prior to the closing or completion date, the Purchaser's lawyer reviews the Purchaser's Mortgage document (which is usually prepared by the Mortgagee's lawyers) and ensures that the Purchaser understands its provisions. An open Mortgage allows the Purchaser to pay off the Mortgage balance at any time, whereas a closed Mortgage does not. There are Mortgages that are semi-open--they have prepayment privileges. The Purchaser's lawyer also ensures that the Purchaser understands the penalties for early repayment or default.

Clients who need legal advice but cannot afford it can apply for legal aid. This means that the client will pay a nominal fee, perhaps $30, and the province will fund the remainder of the lawyer's fees. Obviously, all legal aid applications are carefully reviewed to ensure that the client is really in need of both money and legal advice.

····1····2····3···4···5···6····7····8···9····10····11····12

TIMING 4

Many law firms, both large and small, are highly automated. They have to be in order to keep up with the exceptionally high volume of paperwork. Very few legal documents are keyed only once. The majority of documentation is drafted and amended several times before it leaves the law firm. Word processing is, therefore, a major feature in most law firms. In addition to word processing, many law firms use some form of computerized accounting system so that lawyers' time and disbursements can be calculated and posted to clients' accounts and bills generated with very few keystrokes. Because law firms must organize large numbers of documents for trials, automated systems are also used for litigation support. These systems code and classify documents that the lawyer will need to refer to in court.

Mortgage on the property, this will show on the title search
because the Vendor owes money to the Mortgagee (the lender).

While the title search is being conducted, the Purchaser
will be negotiating a mortgage, if necessary. Sometimes the
Vendor has an existing mortgage with favourable terms that
he or she is prepared to assign to the Purchaser.

When the Purchaser's lawyer has conducted and reviewed the
title search, he or she reports back to the Purchaser. If
everything is in order, the Purchaser's lawyer then proceeds
with the conveyance.

The Purchaser's lawyer contacts the Vendor's lawyer to make
arrangements regarding the conveyance. Usually the Vendor's
lawyer arranges for the discharge of the Vendor's existing
Mortgage on the property and provides the mortgage pay-out
figure to the Purchaser's lawyer as soon as it is available.
The Purchaser's lawyer uses this figure in the preparation
of the Vendor's Statement of Adjustments.

The Purchaser's lawyer then obtains information on property
taxes, etc., and prepares the Transfer document, various
documents required by the local Land Title Office, and the
Purchaser's and Vendor's Statements of Adjustments. The
Statements of Adjustments show the financial adjustments as
at the adjustment date. For example, if the Vendor has paid
property taxes for the entire year, sells the property in
August, and has an adjustment date of August 31, then the

· · · · 1 · · · · 2 · · · · 3 · · · · 4 · · · · 5 · · · · 6 · · · · 7 · · · · 8 · · · · 9 · · · · 10 · · · · 11 · · · · 12

COMPREHENSION 2

Indicate your knowledge of the following terms by using each in a separate sentence. If you are uncertain of any words, use your dictionary.

docket	trust accounts
Retainer Agreement	legal advice
retainer	legal aid
fees	client
disbursements	bar

PARAGRAPH PRACTICE

Read the following paragraphs and then key an accurate copy of each one. If you make any errors, drill each word correctly for one minute.

PARAGRAPH 1

Even though many legal documents are stored in computers in boilerplate form or are generated using forms-processing software, some offices still use printed legal forms. These forms must be completed using a typewriter, and some special procedures must be followed. For example, when completing a printed form, the inserted text must align horizontally and vertically with the pre-printed words. Any small blank spaces should be filled in with a line of dashes (-----). Large blank spaces should be filled with a Z-ruling, using a black ballpoint pen and a

running expenses of the property, such as hydro, cable |498|
television, telephone, property taxes, water rates, etc.; |509|
and the possession date (the date on which the Purchaser |520|
can move into the property). Usually the adjustment and |531|
possession dates are same. |536|

If the Vendor is prepared to accept the Purchaser's offer |547|
(including the subject clauses), then he or she signs the |558|
Contract of Purchase and Sale or Interim Agreement. |568|

As each subject is removed from the Contract of Purchase and |580|
Sale or Interim Agreement, an Amended Contract of Purchase |592|
and Sale or Interim Agreement is prepared by the real estate |604|
agent. |605|

· · · ·1· · · ·2· · · ·3· · · ·4· · · ·5· · · ·6· · · ·7· · · ·8· · · ·9· · · ·10· · · ·11· · · ·12

TIMING 2 (5 or 10 min)

The Purchaser usually takes the signed Contract of Purchase |12|
and Sale or Interim Agreement to a lawyer. The lawyer |23|
reviews the Contract and conducts a title search in the |34|
appropriate Land Title Office. The main objectives of a |45|
title search are to ensure that the Vendor is really the |56|
registered owner of the property and to determine the |67|
charges registered against the title. |74|

A charge is a claim or a right to claim part or all of |85|
a person's property. For example, if the Vendor has a |96|

· · · ·1· · · ·2· · · ·3· · · ·4· · · ·5· · · ·6· · · ·7· · · ·8· · · ·9· · · ·10· · · ·11· · · ·12

ruler, unless the lawyer prefers to have the person signing the document initial beside the last word preceding the blank space. When proofreading these printed forms, double-check to make sure that you have filled in all of the blank spaces with the correct information by reading the entire document — both the pre-printed and inserted text.

PARAGRAPH 2

Legal instruments consist of three parts: the heading, the body, and the ending. The heading of a legal instrument normally specifies the nature of the document and the parties to the document. For example, the following is the heading of an Agreement between two women, one named Monteith and the other, Chenoweth, and a man named Salbaing. Note the capitalization and spacing of the recitals and copy them carefully.

   THIS AGREEMENT made the   day of November, 19-,

BETWEEN:

    KATHLEEN ANDREA MONTEITH, Computer
    Programmer, and MELISSA JANA CHENOWETH,
    Bank Teller, both of 1720-1220 Nelson
    Street, in the City of Halifax, in the
    Province of Nova Scotia,

    (hereinafter called "Monteith" and
    "Chenoweth"),

           OF THE FIRST PART;

company would receive $10,750 plus GST from the Vendor. Seven percent of $100,000 is $7,000 and 2 1/2% of $150,000 is $3,750, making a total of $10,750.

When a prospective Purchaser wants to place an offer on a piece of real property, he or she must leave a deposit with the real estate agent and sign a written Contract called a "Contract of Purchase and Sale" or an "Interim Agreement." Most provinces have standard printed Contract forms that real estate agents use.

In most cases, a Purchaser will only put an offer on a piece of property subject to certain conditions. These conditions should be clearly set out in the Contract of Purchase and Sale. Examples of conditions are that the Purchaser will buy the property subject to selling his or her own home or subject to obtaining financing, such as a Mortgage. Real estate agents usually have a book of conditions clauses that are legally accurate. The Purchaser usually stipulates a time frame within which he or she agrees to remove the subject clauses from the Contract. This time frame may be negotiated back and forth between the Purchaser and the Vendor.

The Contract of Purchase and Sale or the Interim Agreement sets out the completion date (the date on which the registered ownership of the property will pass from the Vendor to the Purchaser); the adjustment date (the date on which the Purchaser will assume responsibility for the everyday

· · · · 1 · · · · 2 · · · · 3 · · · · 4 · · · · 5 · · · · 6 · · · · 7 · · · · 8 · · · · 9 · · · · 10 · · · · 11 · · · · 12

159   LAND, REAL ESTATE, CONVEYANCING

AND:

CLAYTON EDGAR SALBAING, Consultant, of
5467 Montrose Crescent, in the City of
Halifax, in the Province of Nova
Scotia,

(hereinafter called "Salbaing"),

OF THE SECOND PART;

PARAGRAPH 3

When a party to a legal instrument is a company, the recital
is a little different. The following is an example of the
recitals in the heading of an Agreement between a married
couple named Dalzell and Studio 8 Clothing Co. Ltd.

THIS AGREEMENT made the   day of November,
19-,

BETWEEN:

DEREK JAMES DALZELL, Athlete, and
MARILYN PRUDENCE DALZELL, Homemaker,
both of 7632 Avenue Road, in the City
of Winnipeg, in the Province of
Manitoba,

(hereinafter called "the Dalzells"),

OF THE FIRST PART;

AND:

STUDIO 8 CLOTHING CO. LTD., a company
incorporated pursuant to the laws of
the Province of Manitoba, having its
registered office at 3256 Ontario
Avenue, in the City of Winnipeg, in the
Province of Manitoba (Incorporation No.
123,456--May 18, 1965),

(hereinafter called "Studio 8"),

OF THE SECOND PART;

5- OR 10-MINUTE TIMINGS

Read the following passages carefully. Set your speed and accuracy goals and then take either a five- or ten-minute timing on each.

TIMING 1

People who want to buy real property usually contact a real | 12
estate agent. The function of a real estate agent is to | 23
sell real estate for Vendors (sellers) and find real estate | 35
for Purchasers. The real estate agent usually tries to | 46
attract prospective Purchasers by advertising in local | 57
newspapers and holding open houses. You have probably seen | 69
"Open House" signs around your neighbourhood. | 78

The real estate agent charges the Vendor a commission when | 89
the property is sold. The amount of the real estate com- | 100
mission varies with the type of listing. For example, the | 112
real estate commission for an exclusive listing with one | 123
real estate company might be 5%, whereas the commission on | 134
a multiple listing with a series of real estate companies | 145
might be 7%. Often the commission on a multiple listing is | 157
7% on the first $100,000 and 2 1/2% on the balance. | 167

Real estate commission percentages are based on the total | 178
sale price of the property. For example, if a house sold | 189
for $250,000, and the real estate commission was 7% on the | 200
first $100,000 and 2 1/2% on the balance, the real estate | 211

• • • • 1 • • • • 2 • • • • 3 • • • • 4 • • • • 5 • • • 6 • • • • 7 • • • • 8 • • • 9 • • • • 10 • • • • 11 • • • • 12

The lawyer handling the case may refer to the Dalzells as "the Party of the First Part" and Studio 8 as "the Party of the Second Part."

PARAGRAPH 4

The paragraphs (commonly called "clauses" or "provisions") in the body of a legal instrument or court document may be keyed either in a block style (starting at the left margin) or an indented style (starting ten spaces from the left margin). Sometimes a lawyer will request that the first word or words of a clause be keyed in upper case or boldface for emphasis. Usually, clauses are double-spaced with triple-spacing between paragraphs. To speed the process of triple-spacing between paragraphs when using word processing software, you should prepare a macro (stored keystrokes) to effect triple-spacing. The following is an example of a clause in the body of a legal instrument.

WHEREAS there is an Agreement between Suzette and Philippe dated the 9th day of March, 19-;

AND WHEREAS there is an existing . . .

PARAGRAPH 5

The clause that follows the last clause in the body of a legal instrument is called the "testimonium clause." In the following example, the clause beginning with the words "IN WITNESS WHEREOF" is the testimonium clause. The section

4. A Morgage is a lone that enables someone to buy real estate.

5. The act of transfering ownership (title) of property from one person to another is called "conveying."

6. The proccess of land passing back to the crown is known as "echeat."

7. When the husband died, he left his property to his wife for her own use absolute during her lifetime.

8. A subdivision is the division of a large lot of land into smaller pieces, sometimes called "parcels."

9. Do they want to own the property as joint tennants or as tennants in common?

10. The person borrowing money under a Mortgage is called the "Mortagee."

11. A Deed/Transfer is a legal document that transfers the ownership of property from one person to another.

12. The closing date is the date on which the registered ownership of the property passes from the Vender to the Purchaser and the date on which the Vender recieves the procedes of the sale.

Check your accuracy with your instructor. If you made any errors in spelling or terminology, drill each word for one minute.

where the witness places his or her name, address, and occupation is called the "attestation clause."

IN WITNESS WHEREOF the parties hereto have hereunto set their hands and seals the day and date first above written.

SIGNED, SEALED, AND DELIVERED)
IN THE PRESENCE OF:)
)
_____)
Name)
)
_____) _____
Address) ASHLEY KIT WONG
)
_____)
)
)
_____)
Occupation)

SIGNED, SEALED, AND DELIVERED)
IN THE PRESENCE OF:)
)
_____)
Name)
)
_____) _____
Address) JESSICA IVY WONG
)
_____)
)
)
_____)
Occupation)

PARAGRAPH 6

Court documents have various endings; however, an Affidavit (which is a sworn statement filed in court) has a special ending called a "jurat." The following is an example of a jurat.

funds in the trust account to pay out the Vendor, the lawyer | 219
involved can expect to be sued by both the Purchaser and the | 231
Vendor. If the funds have been used for the lawyer's | 242
personal use, the lawyer may be disbarred. | 250

Most law firms prepare an In-Out Statement and/or a Balance | 262
Sheet so that they can see what monies are to be credited to | 274
the trust account and what monies are to be debited from the | 286
trust account. If the In/Out Statement or Balance Sheet | 297
does not balance, then the law firm will have to ascertain | 309
the cause. The In/Out Statement and/or Balance Sheet are | 320
prepared before the completion date and are used as a guide | 332
to check the movement of monies through the trust account on | 344
the completion date. | 348

· · · ·1· · · ·2· · · ·3· · · ·4· · · ·5· · · ·6· · · ·7· · · ·8· · · ·9· · · ·10· · · ·11· · · ·12

COMPREHENSION 3

Read the following sentences carefully. Key each sentence once, correcting all errors in fact, terminology, spelling, grammar, and punctuation. Use your dictionary and office handbook.

1. Real property consists of land, buildings, and all things attacked to the land and buildings that are immovable.

2. Another term for "personal property" are "personal chatels."

3. A civil address is a street or mailing adress.

SWORN BEFORE ME *at the City*)
of Edmonton, in the Province)
of Alberta, this   day of)
September, 19--)
)
)
_____)   JASWINDER PARMJIT
)
A Commissioner for taking)
Affidavits for the Province)
of Alberta)

3-MINUTE TIMINGS

Read the following passages carefully. Set your speed and accuracy goals and then take a three-minute timing on each.

TIMING 1

Most law firms generate vast amounts of paperwork both	12
in the form of correspondence and of documentation. For	23
this reason, many law firms spend considerable sums of money	35
buying state-of-the-art equipment to increase productivity.	47
All correspondence and documentation is a reflection of	59
the quality of the firm. If a letter sent to a client	70
contains errors, the client may wonder how competent the	81
law firm will be in representing him or her. If documen-	92
tation is prepared incorrectly it may be rejected by a	103
Court Registry (court documents) or Land Title Office	114
(conveyancing documents). This could result in significant	126
financial losses to the law firm, as well as the loss of a	138
client.	139

. . . . 1 . . . . 2 . . . . 3 . . . . 4 . . . . 5 . . . . 6 . . . . 7 . . . . 8 . . . . 9 . . . . 10 . . . . 11 12

the law firm then pays out the proceeds of the sale to the | 361
Vendor. An easy way to remember this is: Money in, reg- | 372
ister, money out. | 375

. . . . 1 . . . . 2 . . . . 3 . . . . 4 . . . . 5 . . . . 6 . . . . 7 . . . . 8 . . . . 9 . . . . 10 . . . . 11 12

TIMING 3 (3 min)

The business of transferring ownership of real property from | 12
one person to another is known as "conveyancing." Law firms | 24
specializing in conveyancing are, therefore, acting for | 35
clients who are either buying or selling real property. The | 47
buyer of real property is known as the "Purchaser" or | 58
"Transferee." The seller of real property is known as the | 70
"Vendor" or "Transferor." | 75

Because conveyancing involves large sums of money, law firms | 87
are very careful to ensure that their support staff--legal | 99
secretaries and legal assistants--are properly trained. | 110
One minor error could result in the law firm being sued by | 122
either the Purchaser or the Vendor. | 129

Monies received from the Purchaser and the Purchaser's | 140
Mortgagee must always be placed in a trust account. This | 151
money does not belong to either the Purchaser's lawyer or | 162
the law firm. It is critical that this trust account is | 173
never allowed to become overdrawn. The money is required to | 185
pay out the Vendor, the balance of real estate commission, | 196
etc., on the completion date. If there are insufficient | 207

. . . . 1 . . . . 2 . . . . 3 . . . . 4 . . . . 5 . . . . 6 . . . . 7 . . . . 8 . . . . 9 . . . . 10 . . . . 11 12

Legal correspondence does not vary much from any other | 151
office correspondence, except that the wording may be in | 162
legalese. You may discover some older forms of address | 173
still in use in the legal community, because law is still a | 185
very traditional profession. For example, some lawyers | 196
still like to address letters to other partnerships (law | 207
firms, accounting firms, etc.) using the formal "Messrs." | 218
(plural of "Mr."). The inside address would then be: | 229
Messrs. Patterson, Lovejoy & Co. If "Messrs." is not used, | 241
the inside address would be: Patterson, Lovejoy & Co. | 252
"Mesdames" is used in the same way as "Messrs." but refers | 264
to a partnership consisting entirely of women. Many law | 275
firms now have women partners, so the terms "Messrs." and | 286
"Mesdames" are rarely used. | 291

` . . . .1 . . . .2 . . . .3 . . . .4 . . . .5 . . . .6 . . . .7 . . . .8 . . . .9 . . . .10 . . . .11 . . . .12`

TIMING 2 (3 min)

Another traditional style seen in inside addresses | 11
is the use of "Esq." and "Q.C." The term "Esq." means | 22
"Esquire" and is a term of respect that is placed after a | 33
man's last name instead of placing "Mr." before the name. | 44
You will see the use of "Esq." in many legal journals and | 55
law reports. | 57

"Q.C." stands for "Queen's Counsel" and is an honorary | 69
title. If you wanted to address a lawyer who is a Q.C. in | 81
the traditional manner, the first line of the inside address | 93
would read: P. S. Lovejoy, Esq., Q.C. If you wanted to | 104

` . . . .1 . . . .2 . . . .3 . . . .4 . . . .5 . . . .6 . . . .7 . . . .8 . . . .9 . . . .10 . . . .11 . . . .12`

Most conveyances are handled by either lawyers or notaries. 93
These professionals ensure that the proper conveyancing 104
documents are registered in the Land Title Office on the 115
closing (completion) date. The closing date is the date on 127
which the registered ownership of the property passes from 139
the Vendor to the Purchaser and the date on which the Vendor 151
receives the proceeds of the sale. 158

The lawyer or notary ensures that all of the financial 169
transactions are in order before the conveyancing docu- 180
ments are registered. For example, if mortgage financing 191
is not received by the closing date, the conveyancing 202
documents cannot be registered unless there is a letter 213
of intent from the Mortgagee and a letter of undertaking 224
from the Purchaser's lawyer or notary. 232

If the conveyancing documents were to be registered without 244
a letter of intent and the mortgage monies were not dis- 255
bursed, the registered ownership of the property would pass 267
from the Vendor to the Purchaser but the Purchaser would 278
not have enough money to complete the transaction by paying 290
the Vendor. 292

Law firms ensure that they have a certified cheque from the 304
Purchaser deposited in a trust account, plus a letter of 315
intent from the Purchaser's Mortgagee, before they regis- 326
ter the conveyancing documentation. When the conveyancing 337
documentation has been registered in the Land Title Office, 349

· · · ·1· · · ·2· · · ·3· · · ·4· · · ·5· · · ·6· · · ·7· · · ·8· · · ·9· · · ·10· · · ·11· · · ·12

write to this man using a more modern style, the inside address would read: Mr. P. S. Lovejoy, Q.C. Remember that "Mr." and "Esq." are not used together.

Four other variances in legal correspondence relate to format, special notations, subject lines, and complimentary closings.

Letter Formats: Most law firms use full block letters (all elements begin at the left margin) because they are quicker to prepare. More traditional law offices, however, prefer to use an indented paragraph style. The paragraph indentations may be five or ten spaces. Ten spaces is the more traditional format.

Special Notations: Because of the confidential nature of legal work, many letters and envelopes will be marked PRIVATE AND CONFIDENTIAL or CONFIDENTIAL. Another special notation is WITHOUT PREJUDICE. This notation appears only on the letter, not on the envelope. The WITHOUT PREJUDICE notation means that the contents of the letter cannot be used as evidence in court. Opinion letters (a lawyer's opinion regarding, for example, a court case), offers of settlement, etc., are examples of correspondence that may have the WITHOUT PREJUDICE notation on them.

Subject Lines: Law firms make extensive use of subject lines. It is not unusual to have a three- or four-line subject line containing client names, topic, file numbers, etc.

Land Title Office, landowners are protected from unscrupu- 129
lous people who might try to sell property they did not own. 141
For example, a Land Title Office would not permit a son or 153
daughter to sell his or her parents' home because the 164
parents' names would be on the title to the property. The 176
Land Title Office would ensure that the names of the 186
Transferors on the Transfer document were the same as those 198
of the registered owners on the Title. 206

The only circumstances under which a son or daughter could 218
sell his or her parents' home would be if the parent(s) had 230
drawn up a Power of Attorney, allowing the son or daughter 242
to sell the house on behalf of the parent(s). Under these 254
circumstances, the Power of Attorney would have to be sub- 266
mitted to the Land Title Office with the Transfer 276
documentation. 279

· · · ·1· · · ·2· · · ·3· · · ·4· · · ·5· · · ·6· · · ·7· · · ·8· · · ·9· · · ·10· · · ·11· · · ·12

TIMING 2 (3 min)

The Land Title Office, however, cannot protect landowners 11
from unscrupulous people unless the correct ownership 22
documents are registered with the Land Title Office. For 33
example, if Mrs. Bhatia sells her house to Mr. Ho, Mr. Ho 44
must make sure that the proper Deed/Transfer is registered 56
in the Land Title Office. If this document is not regis- 67
tered, Mrs. Bhatia could fraudulently sell her house to 78
someone else! 81

· · · ·1· · · ·2· · · ·3· · · ·4· · · ·5· · · ·6· · · ·7· · · ·8· · · ·9· · · ·10· · · ·11· · · ·12

Complimentary Closings: The complimentary closings of most | 378
law firm correspondence are similar to those used in other | 390
offices. The name of the law firm is usually keyed in | 401
capital letters, a double space below the closing. | 411

· · · ·1· · · ·2· · · ·3· · · ·4· · · ·5· · · ·6· · · ·7· · · ·8· · · ·9· · · ·10· · · ·11· · · ·12

TIMING 3 (3 min)

Legal documents fall into two categories: legal | 11
instruments and court documents. Legal instruments are | 22
documents that are used for other than court purposes, | 33
which means these documents do not have to be registered in | 45
a Court Registry. Examples of legal instruments are Wills, | 57
Powers of Attorney, Statutory Declarations, Notarial | 67
Certificates, and Agreements. Court documents, on the | 78
other hand, are used for court purposes and are registered | 90
in a Court Registry. Examples of court documents are Writs, | 102
Petitions, Affidavits, and Orders. Whenever you refer to a | 114
specific legal document, whether it is a legal instrument | 125
or a court document, you should use an initial capital | 136
letter. | 137

While the headings on the first page of a legal instru- | 149
ment or a court document vary, the basic format does not. | 160
Usually, the top margin of the first page of a court docu- | 172
ment is 2.5 cm (1 inch) and 4 cm (1½ inches) to 5 cm | 182
(2 inches) for a legal instrument. The left margin is 4 cm | 194
and the bottom margin is 2.5 cm. The only variance to this | 206

· · · ·1· · · ·2· · · ·3· · · ·4· · · ·5· · · ·6· · · ·7· · · ·8· · · ·9· · · ·10· · · ·11· · · ·12

one person to another is called "CONVEYANCING." Most
medium-sized and large law firms have a Conveyancing
Department. Alternatively, the Department may be called the
"Land Department" or the "Real Estate Department."

3-MINUTE TIMINGS

*Read the following passages carefully. Set your speed and accuracy goals
and then take a three-minute timing on each.*

TIMING 1

The Land Title System	4
The term "title" means ownership. If you have title to a	15
piece of property, you own it.	21
In Canada, there are two systems of land registration: the	33
land registry system and the land title system. The land	44
registry system is the older of the two. Whichever system	56
a province uses, the concept is the same. A government-	67
supervised Land Title or Registry Office keeps the original	79
copies of all Deeds/Transfers, Mortgages, and other real	90
estate documents. It also keeps a record of the registered	102
owner(s) of the property.	107
Provided that the correct documents are registered with a	118

· · · ·1· · · ·2· · · ·3· · · ·4· · · ·5· · · ·6· · · ·7· · · ·8· · · ·9· · · ·10· · · ·11· · · ·12

is with Wills, which are bound at the top; therefore, the   217

first page of a Will has a 4-cm top margin. The second page   229

of a court document or legal instrument has a 2.5-cm top   240

and bottom margin and, again, a 4-cm left margin. Wills   251

usually have a 4-cm top margin on the second and successive   263

pages. Most legal documents have page numbers at the top   274

of the second and succeeding pages; however, Wills are   285

generally numbered at the bottom of the page. A special   296

feature of legal documents is that the last page is not   307

numbered. In addition, legal documents usually have   317

backing sheets.   320

. . . .1. . . .2. . . .3. . . .4. . . .5. . . .6. . . .7. . . .8. . . .9. . . .10. . . .11. . . .12

COMPREHENSION 3

Read the following sentences carefully. Key each sentence once, correcting all errors in fact, terminology, spelling, grammar, and punctuation. Use your dictionary or office handbook.

1. Legal instruments and court docments has a 4-cm to 5 top margin, a 4-cm left margin, and a 2.5-cm bottom margin.

2. Winipeg Clothing Co. Ltd. is a company incorporating persuant to the laws of the Province of Saskatewan.

3. Large blank spaces mustbe filled with an X-ruling using a red ballpoint pen and a ruler.

the property and the charges (encumbrances) against the property as at a specific date. Examples of charges against a Title are: Mortgages, Easements, Rights-of-Way, Liens, Judgments, Caveats, etc.

PARAGRAPH 5

A MORTGAGE is a loan that enables someone to buy real property. The legal document naming the parties to the loan is also called a "Mortgage." The person borrowing the money is called the "MORTGAGOR"; the person loaning the money is called the "MORTGAGEE." If you have a problem distinguishing between these terms, try to remember that the word "borrower" has "or" in it and the word "Mortgagor" has "or" at the end of it. Another way of remembering is that the word "lender" has two "e's" in it and the word "Mortgagee" ends with two "e's."

PARAGRAPH 6

A DEED is a legal document that transfers the ownership of property from one person (the Grantor) to another (the Grantee). Each province has its own name for this document; for example, in British Columbia this document is called a "FREEHOLD TRANSFER," or "TRANSFER" for short. The person transferring the property is called the "TRANSFEROR" and the person receiving the property is called the "TRANSFEREE." The act of transferring ownership (title) of property from

4. Studio 8 Clothing Co. Ltd. is the party of the first part.

5. The clauses in the body of a legal instrument maybe keyed either in a block or indented style.

6. Clauses are usually keyed in the single-spacing with double-spacing between paragraphs.

7. The clause that follows the last clause in the body of a legal instrument is called the "testimonium clause."

8. When a witness placexs his or her name, address, and occupation is called the "attestion clause."

9. The legal instrument was signed, seeled, and deliver in presence of Adrienne Lorette Duplessis.

10. She is a commission for taking Affidavits

11. Some law firms still use the formal titles of Messers. and Esqr. when addressing correspondance.

12. The special notation WITH PREJUDICE should appear on both the letter and the envelope.

Check your accuracy with your instructor. If you made any errors in spelling or terminology, drill each word for one minute.

PARAGRAPH 3

All land has some form of LEGAL DESCRIPTION. Although the components of a legal description vary, the following is a typical urban legal description: Lot 12, Block 34, District Lot 235, Group 1, New Westminster District, Plan 13354. Land Title Offices use legal descriptions to identify pieces of property. With the advent of computerization of Land Title Offices, land can now be identified by a PARCEL IDENTIFIER NUMBER (commonly referred to as a "PID" or "PIN"). If you do not know the legal description of a piece of property, you can usually obtain this information from the assessment office of your municipal government by supplying the CIVIC ADDRESS of the property. A civic address is a street or mailing address; for example, 900 Rainbow Road, Whitehorse, Yukon Territory Y1A 3X3.

PARAGRAPH 4

A LANDOWNER is someone who owns real property, holding TITLE to the property. The term "title" means ownership. The term can also be used to refer to the legal document that shows proof of ownership by listing the names of the owners. The full name of this legal document varies from province to province; however, one name is a "CERTIFICATE OF INDEFEASIBLE TITLE." The document usually provides the following information: the full names, occupations, and addresses of the registered owners; the legal description of

5- OR 10-MINUTE TIMINGS

Read the following passages carefully. Set your speed and accuracy goals and then take either a five- or ten-minute timing on each.

TIMING 1

In all legal work, you must be very careful in keying	12
names. The spelling must be correct and you must never	23
change the name in any way. Many people new to the legal	34
field fall into the trap of changing the names of companies.	46
For example, if a company is registered (with the provincial	58
corporate Registry) as "Parnell Enterprises Co. Ltd.," that	70
is the way you must key the name. If you were to key the	81
name as "Parnell Enterprises Company Limited," this would be	93
incorrect. You must, therefore, be alert and never jump to	105
conclusions as far as names are concerned.	113
The way in which names of individuals and companies are	125
keyed in legal correspondence and legal documentation	135
varies. When keying the name of an individual or company in	147
a legal letter, it is usual to use initial capital letters;	159
for example, Sulamith Weygang. If you were keying this name	171
in a legal document, you would normally key the entire name	183
in capital letters; for example, SULAMITH WEYGANG.	193
Capitalization of titles is also commonplace in the	204
legal field. For example, titles such as "Plaintiff,"	214
"Defendant," "Appellant," "Respondent," and "Petitioner"	225
often have initial capitals. When occupations are specified	237

. . . . 1 . . . . 2 . . . . 3 . . . . 4 . . . . 5 . . . . 6 . . . . 7 . . . . 8 . . . . 9 . . . . 10 . . . . 11 12

PARAGRAPH 1

"REAL ESTATE" is another term for "REAL PROPERTY." Real property consists of land, buildings, and all things attached to the land and buildings that are immovable (fixtures). In determining whether an item is a FIXTURE, it must be determined how immovable the article is and whether the article is intended to be a fixture to the property. For example, an area rug would not be considered a fixture; however, wall-to-wall carpeting would, in all probability, be considered a fixture.

PARAGRAPH 2

The term "PERSONAL PROPERTY" refers to all your movable possessions other than real property (land and buildings). Examples of personal property are cars, boats, clothing, jewellery, paintings, etc. Another term for personal property is "PERSONAL CHATTELS." When conveying REAL PROPERTY it is possible to convey PERSONAL PROPERTY too, as in the situation where a Vendor sells his or her house to a Purchaser and agrees to include the washer, dryer, freezer, refrigerator, stove, etc. All of these appliances are PERSONAL PROPERTY.

in legal instruments and court documents, they also often
have initial capitals; for example, SULAMITH WEYGANG,
Architect. Names of legal documents are often capitalized;
for example, Will, Statutory Declaration, Power of Attorney,
Petition for Divorce, Writ of Summons, Appearance, and
Order.

Another area in which capitalization differs is in the
expression of sums of money. When keying legal correspondence it is usual to specify sums of money in figures
alone; for example, $10,999.00. Note that, in legal docu-
ments and correspondence, sums of money are specified
with commas between the hundreds and thousands. You must
not key "$10 999.00," because there is a risk that someone
could insert another figure in the space. When sums of
money are keyed in legal documents, they are spelled out in
full in capital letters and also expressed in figures; for
example, ...TEN THOUSAND, NINE HUNDRED AND NINETY-NINE
($10,999.00) DOLLARS.

Percentages are expressed in a similar manner to sums
of money. In legal correspondence, percentages are keyed in
figures alone; for example, 15%. In legal documentation,
percentages are spelled out in full in capital letters and
also expressed in figures; for example, FIFTEEN (15%)
PERCENT.

Can you put this knowledge into practice? In a legal
letter you would key: "Sulamith Weygang promises to pay

. . . . 1 . . . . 2 . . . . 3 . . . . 4 . . . . 5 . . . 6 . . . . 7 . . . . 8 . . . 9 . . . . 10 . . . . 11 12

a member of the co-operative wants to move, the member sells   106
his or her share to the buyer. The member also turns the   117
Lease over to the new owner.   123

A major difference between co-operative and condominium   134
ownership is the method of sharing expenses. In a condo-   145
minium, the owner of each individual unit (apartment,   156
townhouse, etc.) pays his or her own mortgage, property   167
taxes, etc., whereas in a co-operative, the owner of each   178
unit pays a share of the mortgage and property taxes cover-   190
ing all of the units.   194

· · · ·1· · · ·2· · · ·3· · · ·4· · · ·5· · · ·6· · · ·7· · · ·8· · · ·9· · · ·10· · · ·11· · · ·12

COMPREHENSION 2

Indicate your knowledge of the following terms by using each one in a separate sentence. If you are uncertain of any words, use your dictionary.

zoning   joint tenants

by-law   tenants-in-common

condominium   escheat

fee-simple   Crown

life estate   leasehold

PARAGRAPH PRACTICE

Read the following paragraphs and then key an accurate copy of each. If you make any errors, drill each word correctly for one minute.

$10,999.00 with interest at 15% per annum."   In legal docu- | 520
mentation, you would key: "SULAMITH WEYGANG promises to pay | 532
TEN THOUSAND, NINE HUNDRED AND NINETY-NINE ($10,999.00) | 543
DOLLARS with interest at FIFTEEN (15%) PERCENT per annum. | 554

. . . .1. . . .2. . . .3. . . .4. . . .5. . . .6. . . .7. . . .8. . . .9. . . .10. . . .11. . . .12

TIMING 2 (5 or 10 min)

Legal documents fall into two main categories: legal | 11
instruments and court documents. Legal instruments | 21
are not used for court purposes whereas court | 30
documents are, which means that a court document | 40
is usually filed in a Court Registry whereas a legal | 50
instrument is not. If you are working in civil or | 60
criminal litigation, including family law, you will | 70
be involved in preparing court documents. Some | 79
documents in the Wills and Estates area of law | 88
are also court documents. However, if your lawyer | 98
is not involved in court work, you will be keying | 108
primarily legal instruments. | 114

Examples of common legal instruments are | 123
Agreements, Statutory Declarations, Notarial | 132
Certificates, Powers of Attorney, and Releases. | 141
¶ Agreements, or Contracts, are documents that set | 152
out the terms of an agreement between two or | 161
more parties. The parties can be either individuals | 171
or companies, financial institutions, etc. The names, | 182
addresses, and occupations of the parties are set out | 193

54   WORKING IN A LAW FIRM

etc., as well as a portion of the common areas of the   44
condominium complex. The common areas (common property)   55
normally include swimming pools, recreational/social cen-   66
tres, laundry rooms, elevators, hallways, parking areas,   77
grounds (play areas, gardens, etc.).   84

The owner of the condominium pays his or her own mortgage   95
and property taxes plus a monthly fee to the strata cor-   106
poration. The monthly fee usually covers the maintenance   117
of the grounds, building, etc., as well as the property   128
taxes, insurance, etc., on the common areas.   137

Each strata corporation is set up a little differently, so   149
it is very important for anyone considering buying a condo-   161
minium to read the by-laws of the corporation carefully.   172

· · · ·1· · · ·2· · · ·3· · · ·4· · · ·5· · · ·6· · · ·7· · · ·8· · · ·9· · · ·10· · · ·11· · · ·12

TIMING 4

Another alternative to private ownership of property is to   12
join a co-operative. In a co-operative arrangement, a   23
number of individuals or families form a company to buy a   34
housing complex. Each individual or family then buys shares   46
in the company. The company gives the individual or family   58
a Lease on the portion of the housing complex they want to   70
own.   71

All co-operative members share both the mortgage payment   82
and property tax bill for the entire housing complex. When   94

· · · ·1· · · ·2· · · ·3· · · ·4· · · ·5· · · ·6· · · ·7· · · ·8· · · ·9· · · ·10· · · ·11· · · ·12

in the heading of the Agreement. If any of the parties are other than an individual, such as a corporation, then the address of the registered office of the corporation, together with the incorporation number and date of incorporation, are specified.

The body of the Agreement or Contract sets out the terms that have been agreed to by the parties. The end of the document is signed by all parties to the Agreement or Contract and their signatures are witnessed. Examples of popular types of Agreements or Contracts are Retainer Agreements (which set out the work to be performed by a lawyer, the fees, and the amount of the client's retainer—up-front deposit); Licensing Agreements (which stipulate the rules and regulations under which software companies issue software to customers); Employment Contracts (which outline the terms of employment between an employer and an employee); Marriage or Pre-Nuptial Agreements (which establish the ownership of property prior to and during a marriage); and Separation Agreements (which outline the terms and conditions of a separation between a husband and a wife.

While these Agreements are generally not filed in a Court Registry, a Pre-Nuptial Agreement is normally filed in the Land Title Office if the Agreement contains provisions relating to real

TIMING 2

There are two terms regarding land ownership that
you will encounter regularly in land transactions:
joint tenants and tenants-in-common. When two or
more people decide to buy a piece of property they will
be asked how they want to own the property, as joint
tenants or tenants-in-common.

As joint tenants, when one of the parties dies, the
other owner (irrespective of whether he or she is a
legal heir) automatically inherits the entire property.
This is known as the "right of survivorship."

As tenants-in-common, when one of the parties dies,
the property does not automatically pass to the surviving
person(s).

Individuals buying property with others should consider
very carefully how they want to own the property. If
conveyancing documentation does not indicate that the
parties are joint tenants, then ownership is presumed
to be as tenants-in-common.

TIMING 3

A condominium complex is usually controlled by a strata
corporation. Condominium ownership is the ownership in
fee-simple of a unit, such as an apartment, townhouse,

····1····2····3····4····5····6····7····8····9····10····11····12

property (land/real estate). A Separation Agreement can be filed in a provincial Family Court if the parties so request.

Statutory Declarations are statements of fact that are required for certain government agencies, including Land Title Offices. They are not usually used for court purposes. A person signing a Statutory Declaration is called a "Declarant."

A Notarial Certificate is a document that authenticates another document. For example, if a client required a notarial copy of her Birth Certificate, she would take the original Birth Certificate to her lawyer, who would examine it and then prepare and sign a Notarial Certificate (with a photocopy of the Birth Certificate attached). The Notarial Certificate would state that the attached copy of the Birth Certificate was a true copy of the original Birth Certificate presented to the lawyer.

A Power of Attorney is a document in which someone gives another person (called the "Attorney" — not to be confused with the term "lawyer") authority to act on his or her behalf. These documents are common between family members, especially when an elderly member of the family wants a younger member to handle his or her banking affairs or to act on his or her behalf in the event of a debilitating illness.

Releases are documents that release one

2-MINUTE TIMINGS

Read the following passages carefully. Set your speed and accuracy goals.
Take two-minute timings on each passage.

TIMING 1

Most people who want to buy residential property do not have	12
sufficient money to buy the property outright. They must go	24
to a lending institution (bank, trust company, etc.) and	35
apply for a Mortgage.	39
A Mortgage is a loan that is secured by the property being	51
purchased. The party lending the money is known as the	62
"Mortgagee" and the party applying for the Mortgage is known	74
as the "Mortgagor." The total amount of money borrowed	85
under a Mortgage is called the "principal." Interest is	96
charged on the principal amount of the Mortgage.	106
A fixed-rate Mortgage has an interest rate that is fixed	117
for the term of the Mortgage; for example, one year. At the	119
end of the term, the Mortgagor must negotiate with the	130
Mortgagee to renew the Mortgage at the current interest	141
rate (which may be higher or lower than the rate for the	152
preceding term). A variable-rate Mortgage means that the	163
interest rate varies over the term of the Mortgage.	173

· · · ·1· · · ·2· · · ·3· · · ·4· · · ·5· · · ·6· · · ·7· · · ·8· · · ·9· · · ·10· · · ·11· · · ·12

party from making further claims from another party. For example, if your mother died and left you a gold ring in her Will, when the Executor of the Estate had given you the ring, he or she would ask you to sign a Release so that you could not at a later date come back and say that you never received the gift.

717
727
737
746
756
765
770

TIMING 3 (5 or 10 min)

Examples of court documents are Writs of Summons, Petitions, Notices of Motion, Affidavits, Orders, Statements of Claim, Statements of Defence, Appearances, etc. The documents required for any given court case will vary with the proceedings initiated. One thing is common to all court documents: they must be filed in a Court Registry.

While the formats of court documents vary slightly from province to province, most court documents have a similar heading called a "style of proceeding" or "cause of action." The style of proceeding consists of the action number (court file number), the name of the Court Registry in which the document will be filed, the name of the court in which the document will be presented, and the name of the parties and their titles. The parties' titles are usually "Plaintiff" and "Defendant" or "Petitioner" and "Respondent." If the court document is to be filed in an appeal court, then the titles of the parties will be "Appellant" and "Respondent."

11
23
34
46
58
68
80
91
103
115
126
137
149
160
171
182
194

· · · ·1· · · ·2· · · ·3· · · ·4· · · ·5· · · ·6· · · ·7· · · ·8· · · ·9· · · ·10· · · ·11· · · ·12

Read the following sentences carefully. Key each sentence once.
Concentrate on accuracy and rhythmic keying.

1. The Purchaser is responsible for checking the zoning by-laws.

2. A "strata lot" is also known as a "condominium."

3. Do you want to own your property as joint tenants or tenants-in-common?

4. The Vendor is the registered owner of the property.

5. The lawyer advised him that he was at liberty to rent or sell the property on Drury Lane.

6. A life estate is another form of land ownership.

7. The Planning Department of the municipal government advised her that the area was zoned for single-family dwellings.

8. That area is zoned for industrial parks.

9. This law firm handles hundreds of land transactions per year.

10. A further alternative to either private ownership of property or renting is the co-operative system.

11. A subdivision is the division of a large parcel of land into smaller pieces, sometimes called "lots."

12. When subdividing a parcel of land into more than three lots, a Prospectus usually has to be prepared and approved by the appropriate government department.

The name of the document follows the style of proceeding. It is usually keyed in full capital letters at the centre of the page. The body of the document is then keyed double spaced, with triple-spacing between paragraphs.

The ending of a court document depends on the type of document being prepared; however, most court documents are signed by the Solicitor for the Plaintiff, Defendant, Petitioner, or Respondent. Court Orders, the documents that outline what a Judge has ordered, are signed by the court. The legal term for such signing is "executing."

As with legal instruments, the majority of court documents require backing sheets. While the format of a backing sheet varies from province to province and law firm to law firm, the standard information supplied is the action number; the name of the Court Registry; the name of the court; the names and titles of the parties named in the style of proceeding; the name of the document; the name, address, and telephone number of the lawyer filing the document in court; the initials of the lawyer; and the client file number.

Originally, backing sheets were prepared in landscape mode, with the information keyed in the centre third of the letter-sized backing sheet so that the document could be folded in three and the backing sheet information displayed. If legal-sized paper was used, the backing sheet information was keyed in the second quarter from the left and the document folded to display the backing sheet information on

. . . . 1 . . . . 2 . . . . 3 . . . . 4 . . . . 5 . . . 6 . . . 7 . . . . 8 . . . . 9 . . . . 10 . . . . 11 . . . 12

When you are the registered owner of a piece of property,	11
you own it absolutely. Lawyers call this "holding it in	22
fee-simple." This means that you can rent, sell, or will	33
the property to someone else. You can do virtually any-	44
thing with the property, provided that you do not break the	56
law. Most municipalities have zoning by-laws that stipulate	68
what can be built on the land; for example, single-family	79
dwellings, condominiums, industrial parks, etc.	88

· · · ·1· · · ·2· · · ·3· · · ·4· · · ·5· · · ·6· · · ·7· · · ·8· · · ·9· · · ·10· · · ·11· · · ·12

Did you achieve your speed and accuracy goals on at least one of the timings? If not, repeat the timings.

COMPREHENSION 1

Key the following sentences once, filling in each blank with the appropriate legal term or phrase.

1. The process by which land passes back to the Crown is called ---.

2. A --- is when someone owns land for the duration of his or her life only.

3. --- is the absolute owner of land in Canada.

4. A --- estate means that anyone can inherit the estate.

5. A --- estate has a specific time period attached to it.

6. The most common type of estate is called the ---.

Check your answers with your instructor.

LAND, REAL ESTATE, CONVEYANCING

one quarter. Now that many court documents and legal | 507
instruments are prepared on computerized equipment, it is | 518
often quicker and easier to produce backing sheets with the | 530
information keyed down the page in the normal manner (rather | 542
than in landscape mode); however, this means that the | 553
backing sheet cannot be folded in an attractive manner. It | 565
may be only a matter of time before backing sheets become | 576
obsolete. | 578

When a court document is filed in a Court Registry, | 589
several copies of the document must be presented and any | 600
applicable court filing fees paid. The original document | 611
will be stamped with a court stamp and the date of regis- | 622
tration, and kept in the court files. Copies of the docu- | 634
ment are stamped and returned to the person filing the | 645
document, for its intended purpose, such as for serving or | 657
delivering to other parties, or for filing in the law firm's | 669
files. | 670

· · · ·1· · · ·2· · · ·3· · · ·4· · · ·5· · · ·6· · · ·7· · · ·8· · · ·9· · · ·10· · · ·11· · · ·12

PRODUCTION EXERCISES

EXERCISE 1

Latin terms are contained in many legal documents as well as in legal correspondence. Read the following Latin terms and their English equivalents. Set yourself a production time limit and then key the Latin terms in alphabetical order, together with their meanings, as quickly and accurately as you can.

TIMING 3

Another common form of estate is the leasehold estate. One 12
difference between a fee-simple estate and a leasehold 23
estate is that a leasehold estate has a specific end date 34
attached to it whereas a fee-simple estate may exist over 45
many generations. You have probably seen advertisements 56
for leasehold property in the newspaper; for example, a 99- 68
year Lease. A person who grants a Lease of property to 79
another is called a "Lessor" (landlord). The Lessee is the 91
person who holds an estate by virtue of a Lease (the tenant 103
of a landlord). 106

· · · ·1· · · ·2· · · ·3· · · ·4· · · ·5· · · ·6· · · ·7· · · ·8· · · ·9· · · ·10· · · ·11· · · ·12

TIMING 4

The term "life estate" means that someone owns land for 11
the duration of his or her life only. For example, if a 22
husband died and in his Will left property to his wife 33
for her own use absolutely during her lifetime, but 43
stipulated that his daughter would inherit on the 53
wife's death, the wife could not will the property 63
to anyone. Upon the wife's death, the property would 74
pass to the daughter named in the husband's Will 84
as beneficiary following his wife's death. 92

ad valorem	according to value
ipso facto	by the fact itself
bona fide	in good faith
aliunde	from another source
actus reus	the guilty act (the criminal act)
ab initio	from the beginning
compos mentis	of sound mind
a posteriori	from the latter
de jure	by right
causa	cause
de facto	in fact
mens rea	guilty mind
caveat emptor	let the buyer beware
corpus juris	body of law
de bene esse	conditionally
damnum absque injuria	loss without injury
et seq.	and the following
Regina	queen
ex parte	on behalf of (without the party being present)
actio non	not an action
et non	and not
inter alia	among other things
ex post facto	after the fact
ergo	therefore
ad hoc	for this purpose
factum	deed
infra	below

Read the following paragraphs carefully. Set your speed and accuracy goals. Take one-minute timings on each paragraph.

TIMING 1

The basic theory of land law in Canada, as far as ownership	12
is concerned, is that the Crown (the Government) is the	23
absolute owner of all land. Private citizens, such as you	35
and I, can only own an estate in land. The most common type	47
of estate is called the "fee-simple estate." This term is	59
derived from the word "fee," meaning "inherited," and the	70
word "simple," meaning "anyone."	76

· · · ·1· · · ·2· · · ·3· · · ·4· · · ·5· · · ·6· · · ·7· · · ·8· · · ·9· · · ·10· · · ·11· · · ·12

TIMING 2

The term "fee-simple," therefore, means that an estate	11
can be inherited by anyone, not just the relatives of the	22
deceased owner. What happens if a landowner dies but	33
does not leave a Will or any heirs to his or her estate?	44
The land will revert (go back) to the Crown as the	54
absolute owner. This process of the land passing back	65
to the Crown is known as "escheat."	72

ibid.	in the same place
ignorantia legis non excusat	ignorance of the law is no excuse
et al.	and others
a priori	from the first
in hoc	in reference to this
supra	above
inter vivos	between the living
aliquot	some
in toto	in total
per se	through itself
lis pendens	litigation pending
nemo est supra legis	no one is above the law
per stirpes	by family stock
nunc pro tunc	now for then
obiter dictum	a passing statement
per diem	per day
per annum	per year
vel non	or not
non sequitur	it does not follow
id est (i.e.)	that is
pactum	contract
pro bono	for the good of
prima facie	on the face of it
quo warranto	by what right or authority
absque hoc	without this
quid pro quo	something for something
viz.	namely
res	thing

WORD PRACTICE

Key one line of each of the following words. Concentrate on accuracy and rhythmic keying.

ownership	absolutely
Crown	land
estate	heirs
fee-simple	Government
escheat	inherited
leasehold	deceased
Will	owner
reverts	process
beneficiary	derived
property	landowner

PHRASE PRACTICE

Key each of the following phrases six times. Concentrate on accuracy. Say each phrase to yourself as you key it. Remember to key rhythmically.

absolute owner	for her own use absolutely
an estate in land	the property passes
fee-simple estate	the land reverts
leasehold estate	specific period of time
to his or her estate	the deceased owner

status quo	existing state/situation
in loco parentis	in place of a parent
tempore	for the time of
Rex	king
subpoena	under penalty
sine qua non	without which not
ultra vires	beyond the power (authorized by law)
ex officio	by virtue of his or her office
contra	against

EXERCISE 2

Read the following Promissory Note carefully. Check the document carefully for accuracy, bearing in mind the formatting and style required for a legal instrument. Format the backing sheet in landscape mode. Set yourself a production time limit and then key the material quickly and accurately.

$19,000.00

OTTAWA, ONTARIO

Febuary 6, 19–

PROMISSARY NOTE

I, Blake Rosentzveig, of 7654 Rideau Canal Drive, in the City of Ottawa, in the Province of Ontario, DO PROMISE TO PAY to the order of Rose-Marie Fryett of 2021 Devonshire Bouleyard, in the City of Ottawa, in the Province of Ontario, the sum of Nineteen Thousand, Five Hundred ($19,500) Dollars per month commencing on the 1st day of

Land,
Real Estate,
Conveyancing

March, 19-, together with interest at the rate of Thirteen
(13%) percent per annum.

VALUE RECIEVED   _____

                                    BLAKE ROSENTZVEIG

Backing Sheet

DATED: February 6, 19-

_____

                    BLAKE ROSENTZVEUG

                          TO

                   ROSE-MARIE FRYETT

_____

                    PROMISSARY NOTE

_____

            JULIO CUFFARI, ESQ.
            CUFFARI, ORT, ZULY & CO.
            Barristers and Solicitors
            800-1545 Carling Avenue
            OTTAWA, ONTARIO
            K1Z 8P9

            Tel: (613) 729-5432

_____

JC/(Your initials)   File No. 34,789/5

the Respondent, DANIELLE RIOUX, who were married at Montreal, Quebec, on the 19th day of October, 1965, are divorced from each other, the divorce to take affect on the 20th day of March, 19--.

APPROVED AS TO FORM BY:

_____
Council for the Petitioner

_____
Council for the Respondent

                        BY THE COURT

                        DISTRICT REGISTRAR

Read the following letter carefully, watching for errors. Set yourself a production time limit and then key the letter quickly and accurately. Make all necessary copies and prepare envelopes or envelope labels.

To: Messers. Stuart, Goodman & Co., 419 Adelaide Street, Dalhousie, New Brunswick EOK 1B0
Attention: Ms. D. M. Aylen

WITHOUT PREJUDICE

Re: Purchase by Adanac Cement Ltd. ("Purchaser") from Ward Enterprises Ltd. ("Vendor") of 1654 Mortimer Street, Dalhousie, New Brunswick ("the Transaction")

We are solicitors for the purchaser in the above Transaction and as such have examined the following documents:

1. the Purchase Agreement dated May 18, 19--;
2. the Memorandum and Articles of the Purchaser;
3. the corporate records of the Purchaser;
3. a certified copy of the Resolution of the Board of Directors of the Purchaser approving the Transaction;
4. the Vendor's Mortgages;
5. the Assignment of Permits and Licences;
6. the Assignment of Guaranties, Warranties, and Contractual Obligations; and
7. the Assignment of Approved Service Contracts.

We have also examined such other documents and have

Read the following Divorce Order for a defended divorce with a specified effective date and make sure that you understand it. Key the appropriate style of proceeding/cause of action for your province. Set yourself a production time limit and then key the document quickly and accurately.

Action No./Court File No. D49428

Petitioner: Danielle Rioux

Respondent: Pierre Rioux

DIVORCE ORDER

BEFORE THE HONOURABLE MADAM) WENESDAY, THE 15TH DAY OF
)
JUSTICE ALEONG   ) MARCH, 19--

THIS PROCEDING coming on for trial at (Name of your city and province), on the 15th day of March, 19--; and upon hearing ROSS WARD, Counsel for the Petitioner, and PATRICIA JOE, Counsel for the Respondent, and on hearing the evidence adduced, and the court being of the opinion that by reason of special circumstances the divorce should take effect earlier than the 31th day after this date and the spouses having agreed and undertaken that no appeal will be taken from this Order:

THIS COURT ORDERS that subject to section 12 of the Divorce Act, 1985, the Petitioner, PIERRE RIOUS, and

conducted such investigations and enquiries as we have deemed necessary or adviseable for the rendering of this opinion.

In connection with the opinions hereinafter expressed, we have assumed the corporate status, rights, power, and authority and capacity of all parties other than the Purchaser and we have assumed that the Agreements and instruments covered by the opinions hereinafter expressed which has been entered into by parties other than the Purchaser have been duly authorized, executed, and delivered by and to be valid and legally binding upon such other party or parties.

Based upon the foregoing, we are of the opinion that:

1. The Purchaser is a company duly constituted, organized, and validly existing under the laws of the Province of New Brunswick and is in good standing with respect to the filing of Annual Reports in the Office of the New Brunswick Director of Corporate Affairs.

2. The Purchaser has the corporate capacity and power to enter into, execute, and deliver each of the following documents:

   (a) the Purchase Agreement;

   (b) the Assignment of Permits and Licences

   (c) the Assignment of Guaranties, Warranties, and Contractual Obligations; and

   (d) the Assignment of Approved Service Contracts

   and to perform each and all of the matters and things provided for in each of such Agreements and

diverse places, and in particular the said Respondent and HELEN KACZUR have committed adultry at 4598 Elm Street, in the City of Saskatoon, in the Province of Saskatchewan, and did so commit adultry at that address on or about the 4th day of of January, 19--, and on other occasions better known to the Respondent and the said HELEN KACZUR than to the Petitioner.

RECONCILIATION

3.   All previous attempts to effect reconciliation have failed. There is no possibility of reconciliation or resumtion of cohabitation.

PARTICULARS OF MARRIAGE

4.   Date of marriage: June 5, 1982

5.   Place of Marriage: Sydney, New Zealand

6.   Surname of Wife before marriage: DIEWOLD

7.   Maiden surname of Wife: RICARD

8.   Martial status of Husband at time of marriage:
Bachelor

8.   Marital status of Wife at time of marriage:
        Divorced

9.   A Certificate of Marriage is filled with this
        Petition.

instruments to be performed by it.

3. Each of the documents referred to in paragraph 2 above has been duly authorized, executed, and delivered by the Purchaser and constitutes a legal, valid, and binding obligation of the Purchaser enforceable in accordance with its terms, except that:

(a) enforceability may be limited by bankrupcy, insolvency, or other laws generally affecting the enforcement rights of creditors; and

(b) specific performance is an equitable remedy which may not be available in any particular instance.

4. No consent authorization, licence, franchice, permit, approval, or Order of any court or government agency or body is required for the acquisition by the Purchaser of the purchased property.

Yours very truly

HEENAN, HAMATAKE & CO.

J. B. Hamatake

JBH / (Your initials)

Copy to: Mrs. P. M. Riise, President, Adanac Cement Ltd., 103 Brunswick Street, Dalhousie, New Brunswick EOK 1BO

Adapted from Appendix 14 of *Buying and Selling Commercial Property*. The Continuing Legal Education Society of British Columbia, February 1985.

Read the following portion of a Divorce Petition, watching for errors. Set yourself a production time limit and then key the Petition quickly and accurately.

CLAIMS AND GROUNDS

1.   The Petitioner claims:

(a)   a divorce from the Respondent spouse;

(b)   custody of the infant children of the marriage, namely, KYLE RAVNIC and BRENT HAMILTON RAVNIC;

(c)   support for each of the infant children of the marriage, namely, KYLE RAVNIC and BRENT HAMILTON RAVNIC, in the amount of FOUR HUNDRED AND FIFTY ($450.00) DOLLARS per month; and

(d)   costs against the Respondent, WAYNE ROY RAVNIC.

2.   The Petitioner alleges that there has been a breakdown of the marriage under The Divorce Act, 1985, section 10(2)(b)(i), the particulars of which are as follows:

That since the celebration of the marriage the Respondent has committed adultery with HELEN KACZUR on various and diverse occasions, at various and

Civil Law and Litigation

in the Province of British Columbia, on Wednesday, the 20th
day of August, 19--, at the hour of 8/00 o'clock in the
forenoon, by delivering to and leaving with the said JENIFER
ELEN LANDER personnally, a sealed copy thereof.

2.   A copy of the Petition is annexed and marked
Exhibit "A" to this my Affidavit.

3.   THAT now produced and shown to me and marked
Exhibit "B" to this my Affidavit, is a photograph of
JENNIFER ELLEN LANDER, which is a true likeness of the
person whom I served as aforesaid.

4.   THAT at the time of service of the Petition on
JENNIFER ELLEN LANDER she admitted to me that she was was
the Respondant named therein and the proper party to be
served.

SWORN BEFORE ME at the City   )
of Vancouver, in the Province   )
of British Columbia, this 24th   )
day of August, 19--   )
)
)
_____)   AJAID DHINJAL
A Commissioner for taking   )
Affidavits for British   )
Columbia

WORD PRACTICE

Key one line of each of the following words. Concentrate on accuracy and rhythmic keying.

limitation	Writ
Plaintiff	Tortfeasor
Defendant	wrongdoing
action	tort
contract	negligence
compensation	dispute
jurisdiction	intentional
proceeding	contractual
claim	court
sued	relief

PHRASE PRACTICE

Key each of the following phrases six times. Concentrate on accuracy. Say each phrase to yourself as you key it. Remember to key rhythmically.

limitation period
the Plaintiff's claim against the Defendant
intentional tort
the wrongdoer or Tortfeasor
breach of contract
action commenced by Writ of Summons
the relief sought
contractual obligations
sued for negligence
paying damages

PRODUCTION EXERCISES

EXERCISE 1

Read the following Affidavit of Service, watching for errors. Set yourself a
production time limit and then key the Affidavit (without a backing sheet)
quickly and accurately.

1"

Court file no 12345 > Flush Right

NO. 12345
DS
VANCOUVER REGISTRY

1.5

ONTARIO COURT (GENERAL DIVISION
(center) IN THE SUPEME COURT OF BRITISH COLUMBIA

DS
(CAP) BETWEEN: o.k.

DS
(center)(CAP) ROBERT WILLIAM LANDER,
DS
PETITIONER, Flush right

DS
AND: (center) ———>
— ∧ and ∧ —
JENNIFER ELLEN LANDER,
DS
RESPONDENT, Flush right

DS
AFFIDAVIT OF SERVICE (center)(AllCAP)

DS
10 ——> I, AJAIB DHINJAL, of 1145 Howe Street, in the

Toronto   ONTARIO,
City of Vancouver, in the Province of British Columbia,
Process Server, MAKE OATH AND SAY:

DS
1.   THAT a sealed copy of the Petition herein, dated
23rd   September
the 13th day of August, 1999, against JENNIFER ELEN LANDER
was duly served by me on the said JENNIFER ELEN LANDER at
                                                    NorTH York
702-1567 Bellwood Crescent, in the Muncipality of Burnaby,

133   FAMILY LAW

1-MINUTE TIMINGS

Read the following paragraphs carefully. Set your speed and accuracy goals. Take one-minute timings on each paragraph.

TIMING 1

There are three common branches of civil law: tort law,   11
contract law, and property law. Tort law constitutes a very   23
large portion of civil law. A tort is a wrongdoing for   34
which an injured party may seek compensation from the   45
wrongdoer (Tortfeasor). The most common form of tort is   56
negligence. Another form of tort is an intentional tort.   67

. . . .1. . . .2. . . .3. . . .4. . . .5. . . .6. . . .7. . . .8. . . .9. . . .10. . . .11. . . .12

TIMING 2

If two or more people are parties to an Agreement or   10
Contract and one of the parties does not abide by the terms   22
of the Agreement or Contract, then the other party or   33
parties can launch a civil action for breach of contract.   44
While a wrongdoing has taken place and the "injured" party   56
will seek compensation for breach of contract, this is not   68
considered to be a tort.   73

. . . .1. . . .2. . . .3. . . .4. . . .5. . . .6. . . .7. . . .8. . . .9. . . .10. . . .11. . . .12

Order, submits it to the Respondent's lawyer for approval, and then files it in court. The court then issues the Order. Once the Divorce Order has been issued by the Court, the Petitioner and Respondent usually have to wait for thirty-one days until the Order becomes effective. This allows time for appeal.

Under some circumstances a court can issue a Divorce Order that is effective immediately or on a specified date prior to the usual thirty-one-day waiting period; however, under s.12(2)(b) of the Divorce Act, 1985, the spouses must agree and undertake that they will not appeal the judgment.

As soon as the effective date of the divorce is reached, the marriage is officially dissolved and a Certificate of Divorce can be obtained from the Court Registry. This Certificate, or a certified copy of it, is conclusive proof that the divorce is effective. At this time, the Petitioner and Respondent are free to remarry if they so desire.

TIMING 3

The main difference between tort law and contract law is | 11
that the parties in tort law have not entered into any | 22
contractual obligations. All of us have tort obligations, | 34
whether we like it or not. Parties in contract law have | 45
thought about their contractual obligations and have usually | 57
signed a document agreeing to the Contract terms. No | 68
Contracts or Agreements are involved in tort law actions. | 79

. . . . 1 . . . . 2 . . . . 3 . . . . 4 . . . . 5 . . . 6 . . . 7 . . . . 8 . . . . 9 . . . .10 . . . .11 12

TIMING 4

Some acts are considered to be both a crime and a tort; for | 12
example, motor vehicle accidents. If someone drives danger- | 24
ously and injures someone, the driver could be convicted of | 36
dangerous driving by the state (a crime) and be subject to | 47
punishment (jail/fine). The driver could also be sued by | 58
the injured party in a tort action and be subject to paying | 70
damages (money) to the injured party. | 77

. . . . 1 . . . . 2 . . . . 3 . . . . 4 . . . . 5 . . . 6 . . . . 7 . . . . 8 . . . . 9 . . . .10 . . . .11 12

TIMING 5

Criminal suits and tort actions, even if they arise | 10
from the same incident, are tried separately. | 19
Criminal suits are initiated by the Crown and the | 29
accused is prosecuted in criminal court. Tort actions | 40

and no court appearance will be necessary.

In most provinces, the court in which the divorce is processed requires the Respondent to produce some form of financial statement if child support or custody is involved. If the Respondent wants to dispute some relief sought by the Petitioner in the Petition for Divorce, he or she arranges for an Answer to be filed and delivered to the Petitioner or Petitioner's lawyer. If the Respondent wants to sue the Petitioner for divorce, a Counter-Petition is filed in the Court Registry and served on the Petitioner.

An Answer and Counter-Petition is used when the Respondent wants to dispute some relief sought by the Petitioner or to sue the Petitioner for divorce. In certain circumstances a Respondent may prepare a Notice of Intent to Defend.

A defended divorce action follows the same procedure as any civil litigation case. A trial date is obtained, examinations for discovery are held, and a Trial Record is prepared and filed in court. Throughout this process, efforts may be made to settle out of court to prevent a trial; however, if a settlement is not forthcoming, the case goes to trial.

The Petitioner and the Respondent appear in court. Evidence is submitted by Affidavit or by witnesses present at trial. At the conclusion of the trial the Judge presents either an oral or a written judgment. The Petitioner's lawyer normally prepares the appropriate defended Divorce

are initiated by the injured party (the Plaintiff) who   51

sues the wrongdoer (the Defendant) in civil court.   61

The Plaintiff commences an action against the   70

Defendant by issuing a Writ of Summons, Notice   79

of Action, or similar document, within the time   88

limit stipulated by law. This time limit is called   98

the "limitation period." The Writ sets out the   107

claims against the Defendant and the relief sought.   117

Did you achieve your speed and accuracy goals on at least one of the timings? If not, repeat the timings.

COMPREHENSION 1

Key the following sentences once, filling in each blank with the appropriate legal term or phrase.

1. The three common branches of civil law are --- law, --- law, and --- law.

2. The most common form of tort is ---.

3. The --- must commence an action against the --- by issuing a ---.

4. The time limit within which an action must be commenced is called ---.

5. Another term for "wrongdoer" is ---.

6. If there is a --- of a Contract, the parties to the Contract will seek --- under --- law.

Check your answers with your instructor.

who is unable to look after himself or herself because of | 508
illness or disability (s.2 of the Divorce Act, 1985). It is | 520
essential, therefore, that all references to children in | 531
both the Petition for Divorce and supporting Affidavits | 542
must relate to children under sixteen. | 550

If the documentation presented to the court in an | 561
undefended divorce action is in order, the court will grant | 573
a divorce and issue a Divorce Order. Under s.12(1) of the | 585
Divorce Act, the divorce will take effect on the thirty- | 596
first day after the day on which the judgment granting the | 608
divorce is rendered (unless special circumstances exist). | 619

····1····2····3····4····5····6····7····8····9····10····11····12

TIMING 3 (5 or 10 min)

When the Respondent in a divorce action is served with | 12
the Petition for Divorce, he or she has a time limit in | 23
which to decide what to do. Usually the time limit is 20 | 34
days if the Respondent is served in the same province in | 45
which the Petitioner resides, 40 days if the Respondent is | 57
served in another province or in the United States of | 68
America, and 60 days if the Respondent is served outside | 79
Canada or the United States of America. | 87

Usually a Respondent seeks legal advice when served | 98
with a Petition; however, this is not mandatory. If the | 109
Respondent agrees to the claims in the Petition, then he or | 121
she does nothing. This means that the divorce is undefended | 133

····1····2····3····4····5····6····7····8····9····10····11····12

SENTENCE PRACTICE

Read the following sentences carefully. Key each sentence once.
Concentrate on accuracy and rhythmic keying.

1. If the Plaintiff is claiming a small amount of money from the Defendant, the case will normally be heard in Small Claims Court.

2. Because the claims in Small Claims Court are so small, the parties may represent themselves in court, rather than hire a lawyer to represent them.

3. If the Plaintiff's claim against the Defendant is in excess of about $5,000 but under about $50,000, the case is normally heard in the provincial County Court.

4. When claims against a Defendant are in excess of $50,000, the case is normally heard in a superior court, such as the provincial Supreme Court.

5. The Plaintiff must have a valid claim in law (a cause of action) before commencing a law suit.

6. The Plaintiff cannot commence an action against the Defendant if the limitation period has expired.

7. Under civil law, a corporation is considered to be a legal entity and can either sue or be sued (i.e., a company can be either a Plaintiff or Defendant in a civil action).

If the divorce is undefended, the Petitioner's lawyer will prepare the necessary documentation required by the court. This documentation will vary from province to province; however, it usually consists of the original Affidavit of Service, showing that the Petition for Divorce was served; an Affidavit of the Lawyer to the effect that no Answer or Counter-Petition was filed, served, or delivered; and, if there are children of the marriage, either an Affidavit or a Statement outlining the details of access, custody, and support, as well as details of the financial situations of both spouses.

The objective behind having these Affidavits is to provide the court with sufficient data to make a decision. Since the parties to an undefended divorce do not necessarily have to appear in court, the information that would have been elicited in court must be provided in written form. Obviously, if the court decides that there is insufficient information or wants to question either party, then a hearing will be arranged.

The Divorce Act also places the burden on the court to ensure that the best interests of the children of the marriage are always considered. The court requires specific information relating to the children in order to make decisions that are in the children's best interests.

It is important to note that, for the purposes of divorce, a child of a marriage refers to a child under the age of sixteen or a child of sixteen years of age or over

8. There are two types of proceedings: an action and an originating application.

9. An action is commenced with a document usually called a "Writ," "Writ of Summons," or "Notice of Action."

10. A Writ of Summons names the Plaintiff and Defendant and sets out the Plaintiff's claims against the Defendant.

11. The Plaintiff's claims against the Defendant are usually set out in a general endorsement on the Writ of Summons and expanded on at a later date in another document called a "Statement of Claim."

12. A Writ of Summons must be filed in the appropriate Court Registry before it is served on the Defendant.

2-MINUTE TIMINGS

Read the following passages carefully. Set your speed and accuracy goals. Take two-minute timings on each paragraph.

TIMING 1

When a person decides to sue another person for a	11
wrongdoing, he or she normally consults a lawyer. The	22
lawyer listens carefully to the client's complaints, makes	34
notes on the details of the wrongdoing, and then considers	46
the matter.	48

· · · · 1 · · · ·2 · · · ·3 · · · ·4 · · · ·5 · · · ·6 · · · ·7 · · · ·8 · · · ·9 · · · ·10 · · · ·11 · · · ·12

Respondent is believed to be residing. The rules and procedures relating to substitutional service are set out in each province's Rules of Court or Civil Procedure.

480
491
502

TIMING 2 (5 or 10 min)

When the Petitioner's lawyer receives an Affidavit of Service from the person who served the Petition for Divorce on the Respondent, a record will be made of the limitation date. The Petition for Divorce stipulates the length of time the Respondent has (from the time the Petition was served on him or her) to prepare either an Answer or a Counter-Petition.

If the Respondent replies to the Petition with an Answer, it means that he or she wants to contest the divorce or requires some clarification or minor change to, perhaps, access or custody provisions.

If the Respondent replies to the Petition with a Counter-Petition, it means that the Respondent is suing the Petitioner and, unless a settlement can be negotiated, there is every possibility that the divorce will be a defended one. This means that the parties will have to appear in court.

If the Respondent ignores the Petition, the divorce is regarded as undefended and, therefore, there is little likelihood that a court appearance will be required.

12
24
36
47
58
69
72
83
95
107
113
124
136
148
159
170
171
183
195
204

· · · · 1 · · · · 2 · · · · 3 · · · · 4 · · · · 5 · · · · 6 · · · · 7 · · · · 8 · · · · 9 · · · · 10 · · · · 11 · · · · 12

A lawyer does not immediately commence a lawsuit on behalf of a client. Many different things have to be taken into consideration. Does the client have a case? If the lawyer thinks that the client does, research will be conducted to see what the outcome was of previous cases similar to the client's. If previous cases did not stand up in court, then there is no point in commencing an action.

Another consideration is the cost of launching an action. Does the client have sufficient funds if the case is not successful in court? Yet another consideration is whether the client will be able to collect damages from the Defendant if the Defendant is found liable.

	59
	71
	83
	94
	106
	118
	129
	140
	152
	163
	175
	184

· · · · 1 · · · · 2 · · · · 3 · · · · 4 · · · · 5 · · · · 6 · · · · 7 · · · · 8 · · · · 9 · · · · 10 · · · · 11 · · · · 12

TIMING 2

Once a client has decided to commence an action, the lawyer prepares a Writ of Summons or a similar document. A Writ of Summons is the initial document that commences an action. It sets out the names of the parties to the action: the Plaintiff and the Defendant. The Plaintiff or Defendant may be an individual, a corporation, an estate, etc.

The Writ usually has a general endorsement that sets out the claims of the Plaintiff against the Defendant. If the claims are very brief, the general endorsement can be substituted by a Statement of Claim. In most circumstances, however, the lawyer prepares a general endorsement and then,

	11
	23
	34
	46
	58
	68
	79
	91
	102
	114
	126

· · · · 1 · · · · 2 · · · · 3 · · · · 4 · · · · 5 · · · · 6 · · · · 7 · · · · 8 · · · · 9 · · · · 10 · · · · 11 · · · · 12

in a provincial court; however, it is transmitted to the Central Divorce Registry in Ottawa, where a check is made to ensure that duplicate divorce actions have not been commenced in different provinces.

Once the Petition for Divorce has been signed by the Petitioner, the Registration of Divorce form has been completed, and a Certificate of Marriage or certified copy of the Registration of Marriage has been obtained, the documentation is filed in the provincial Supreme or Superior Court or Court of Queen's Bench, together with the appropriate filing fee. The court then issues the Petition of Divorce and the Petitioner's lawyer can arrange for service on the Respondent and, in the case of adultery, on the Person Named or Co-Respondent.

Because divorce matters come under the umbrella of civil litigation (one individual suing another), the procedures for service are the same as for any other civil litigation case. With divorce matters it is more common for the Respondent to try to evade service. It is not unusual, therefore, for a lawyer to have to make application to court for an Order for Substitutional Service. Substitutional service can be effected by means of serving a close family member, posting a copy of the Petition for Divorce in the Court Registry, or placing a Notice in a local newspaper in the area in which the

at a later stage, prepares a more substantial Statement of
Claim. At this point, neither the court nor the Defendant
are aware that the Plaintiff is commencing an action.

Once the Writ has been prepared and signed by the
Plaintiff's lawyer, it is filed in the appropriate local
Court Registry. The Court Registry charges a filing fee.

. . . . 1 . . . . 2 . . . . 3 . . . . 4 . . . . 5 . . . . 6 . . . . 7 . . . . 8 . . . . 9 . . . . 10 . . . . 11 12

TIMING 3

At the Court Registry, the original and copies of the
Writ of Summons presented by the law firm are stamped with
the court stamp. The original Writ is retained by the court
for its files. The court stamps an action number at the top
of the Writ. This action number is the court file number
and must be quoted on all legal documentation relating to
the action, whether the documents are prepared by the
Plaintiff or the Defendant.

The stamped copies of the Writ are returned to the law
firm so that the law firm can arrange for a copy of the Writ
to be served on the Defendant or Defendants. Usually the
law firm arranges for the Writ to be served on the Defendant
by either a Sheriff or Process Server. If the Defendant is
a corporation, some provincial Court Rules allow the Writ to
be served by double-registered mail to the registered office
of the corporation.

. . . . 1 . . . . 2 . . . . 3 . . . . 4 . . . . 5 . . . . 6 . . . . 7 . . . . 8 . . . . 9 . . . . 10 . . . . 11 12

Read the following passages carefully. Set your speed and accuracy goals and then take either a five- or ten-minute timing on each.

TIMING 1

While the Divorce Act, 1985, outlines the law	10
regarding divorce, each province has rules that stipulate	21
the procedures to be followed to carry out the provisions	33
of this Act. Some procedures, however, are virtually	44
standard in each province. For example, before a	54
Petition for Divorce is filed in the court, the	63
Petitioner must provide proof of marriage. A	72
Petitioner cannot divorce someone to whom he or she	82
is not married. Usually the Petitioner has a copy	92
of the Certificate of Marriage; however, if he or she	103
does not, a certified copy of the registration of	113
Marriage form can be obtained from the provincial	123
government (usually the Department of Vital	132
Statistics) provided the marriage took place in the	142
province. If the marriage was solemnized outside	152
the province or country, then application will have	162
to be made to the local authorities in the location	172
of marriage.	174
Another standard procedure is that any	183
Petition for Divorce should be accompanied by a	192
Registration of Divorce form. This form is filed	202

If a Defendant finds out that he or she is about to be | 12
served with a Writ, that person may try to evade service. | 23
Alternatively, the Sheriff or Process Server may be unable | 35
to locate the Defendant. Under these circumstances, the | 46
Plaintiff's lawyer may have to apply to the court for an | 57
Order for Substitutional Service. | 64

Substitutional service means that the Defendant may | 75
be served by other means than by the Sheriff or Process | 86
Server placing the Writ in the Defendant's hands. Examples | 98
of substitutional service are serving a close family member, | 110
posting the Writ in the Court Registry, placing a copy of | 121
the Writ in the local newspaper in the area in which | 131
the Defendant resides, or even nailing the Writ to the | 142
Defendant's front door! | 147

A Judge will not automatically grant an Order for | 158
Substitutional Service and may ask the Plaintiff's lawyer to | 170
continue to try to effect personal service on the Defendant. | 182

• • • •1• • • •2• • • •3• • • •4• • • •5• • • •6• • • •7• • • •8• • • •9• • • •10• • • •11• • • •12

COMPREHENSION 2

Indicate your knowledge of the following terms by using each one in a separate sentence. If you are uncertain of any words, use your dictionary.

Plaintiff   Statement of Claim

Defendant   action number

5. Three major bars to obtain a divorce are: colusion, condonation, and connivence.

6. The person sueing for divorce is known as the Respondant.

7. A third party being sued for damages in a divorce proceding is known as a Co-Respondant.

8. Custody and assess arrangement are outlined in the Petiton for Divorce.

9. The Agreement was executed without any undue influence or coercion.

10. The infant child of the marriage will be in the care and control of the Wife until the said child attains the age of nineteen years, dies, marries, or otherwise becomes self-supporting.

11. The Wife will pay to the Husband for the support of the infant child of the marriage the sum of THREE HUNDRE AND FIFTY ($355.00) DOLLARS.

12. If there has been any reconciliations with a duration in excess of sixty days, then the seperation period must be calculated from the date of the cessation of the last reconciliation.

Check your accuracy with your instructor. If you made any errors in spelling or terminology, drill each word for one minute.

Writ of Summons   substitutional service

damages   limitation period

general endorsement   Court Registry

PARAGRAPH PRACTICE

Read the following paragraphs and then key an accurate copy of each one. If you make any errors, drill each word correctly for one minute.

PARAGRAPH 1

A WRIT OF SUMMONS stipulates the length of time the

Defendant has to advise the Plaintiff that he or she wants

to defend the action. Usually the time period is seven days

if the Defendant lives in the same province as the

Plaintiff; 21 days if he or she lives outside the province

but within Canada; 28 days if the Defendant lives in the

United States of America; and 42 days if the Defendant lives

in another country. Usually the Defendant will seek legal

advice on being served with a Writ of Summons; however, he

or she does not have to. If the Defendant wants to defend

the action, he or she should arrange for a document called

an "APPEARANCE" to be prepared, filed in court, and

delivered to the Plaintiff or the Plaintiff's lawyer within

the limitation period stipulated in the Writ. If the

Defendant does not want to defend the action, he or she does

being made. For example, s.8(2)(a) relates to separation, | 224
s.8(2)(b)(i) relates to adultery, and s.8(2)(b)(ii) relates | 236
to physical or mental cruelty. | 242

The background circumstances to the divorce appli- | 253
cation, the relief sought (maintenance and/or support | 264
for the spouse and the children), and custody and access | 275
arrangements are also outlined in the Petition for Divorce. | 287

The Petitioner signs the Petition and it is then filed | 299
in the provincial Supreme or Superior Court, or Court of | 310
Queen's Bench, depending on the provincial court structure. | 322

· · · ·1· · · ·2· · · ·3· · · ·4· · · ·5· · · ·6· · · ·7· · · ·8· · · ·9· · · ·10· · · ·11· · · ·12

COMPREHENSION 3

Read the following sentences carefully. Key each sentence once, correcting all errors in fact, terminology, spelling, grammar, and punctuation. Use your dictionary and office handbook.

1. The Husband and Wife each acknowledge that he or she has recieved independent legal advise.

2. Under The Divorce Act, 1987, the only ground for separation is marriage breakdown.

3. The adulterous spouce has admitted to commiting adultery.

4. If mental or pyhsical cruelty has taken place, the the lawyer will want to obtain the details of the alledged cruelty.

nothing. When the limitation date for the delivery of an Appearance has expired, the Plaintiff's lawyer will file a DEFAULT JUDGMENT in the court. This means that the Plaintiff has won the case by default.

PARAGRAPH 2

If the Defendant files and delivers an Appearance to the Plaintiff or the Plaintiff's lawyer within the required time frame, the action enters the next stage, called the "pleadings stage." Pleadings are the set of documents prepared by both sides that present the facts and issues of the case. The pleadings stage can be likened to a game of tennis, in that first one side presents a document and then the other side. Once the Defendant has delivered an Appearance, the Plaintiff prepares a STATEMENT OF CLAIM, which outlines the facts and issues of the case and what relief is being sought. Once the Defendant has received and perused the Statement of Claim, he or she arranges for a STATEMENT OF DEFENCE to be prepared. This document defends claims made by the Plaintiff. If the Defendant does not produce a Statement of Defence within the set limitation period, the Plaintiff can prepare a DEFAULT JUDGMENT and "win" the case.

While collusion is an absolute bar to the granting | 210
of a divorce by the court, condonation and connivance | 221
are not. This means that if condonation or connivance | 232
have taken place, the court may grant the divorce if it | 243
feels the divorce would best serve the public interest. | 254

TIMING 3 (3 min)

Under s.9(1) of the Divorce Act, 1985, it is the duty | 12
of every barrister, solicitor, lawyer, or advocate acting | 23
on behalf of a party who wants to commence divorce proceed- | 35
ings, to discuss the possibilities of reconciliation and to | 47
provide information on available marriage counselling or | 58
guidance services. This duty does not have to be fulfilled | 70
if the circumstances are such that it would not be appro- | 82
priate to do so. | 85

The divorce process is usually commenced by the prep- | 97
aration of a document called a "Petition for Divorce." | 108
A Petition for Divorce names the parties involved: the | 119
person suing for divorce is called the "Petitioner" and the | 131
person being sued for divorce is called the "Respondent." | 142
If adultery has occurred, the name of the third party (if | 153
known) will be stated. This third party is known as the | 164
"Person Named." If the Petitioner wants to sue the third | 175
party for damages, then the third party is called the "Co- | 187
Respondent." | 189

The Petition for Divorce also states the section of | 200
the Divorce Act under which the application for a divorce is | 212

· · · ·1· · · ·2· · · ·3· · · ·4· · · ·5· · · ·6· · · ·7· · · ·8· · · ·9· · · ·10· · · ·11· · · ·12

PARAGRAPH 3

Often a Statement of Claim and Statement of Defence are the only documents required to set out the facts and issues; however, other pleadings include a REPLY prepared by the Plaintiff, a REJOINDER prepared by the Defendant, a SURREJOINDER prepared by the Plaintiff, a REBUTTER prepared by the Defendant, and a SURREBUTTER prepared by the Plaintiff. Most provincial Court Rules stipulate that these further pleadings can be prepared only with the sanction of the court (i.e., a COURT ORDER). The reason is that the court wants the Plaintiff and Defendant to get the facts and issues settled as quickly as possible so that time and money are not wasted. At any stage during the pleadings, the Plaintiff and Defendant can attempt to settle out of court. This means that the parties agree to a settlement without the necessity of going to court. This is a very attractive alternative if legal fees are rising and the waiting list to get into court is long.

PARAGRAPH 4

When the pleadings stage has closed, each side in the action usually requests a LIST OF DOCUMENTS from the other side. As the name implies, this is a list of the documents held by the opposing side that are relevant to the case. These documents may include letters, memoranda, telephone messages, accounting documents, Contracts, etc. Once the list of

If mental or physical cruelty has taken place, the
lawyer will want to obtain details of the alleged cruelty,
often in the form of medical reports from hospital emergency
rooms, family doctors, psychologists, or psychiatrists.

218 229 241 252

· · · · 1 · · · · 2 · · · · 3 · · · · 4 · · · · 5 · · · · 6 · · · · 7 · · · · 8 · · · · 9 · · · · 10 · · · · 11 · · · · 12

TIMING 2 (3 min)

There are three major bars to obtaining a
divorce: collusion, condonation, and connivance.

Collusion occurs when a couple agrees to
fabricate or suppress evidence or to deceive the court
in order to obtain a divorce. An example of this
would be if a couple agreed to lie about their
separation date in order to obtain an earlier divorce.

Condonation refers to one spouse forgiving the
other for a particular act; for example, a husband
forgiving his wife for having committed adultery.
There are three essential elements of condonation:
(1) the innocent spouse must have full knowledge
of the circumstances of the offence; (2) the innocent
spouse must intend to forgive the offence; and (3)
the innocent spouse must reinstate the guilty spouse
to his or her former marital position.

Connivance refers to one spouse causing or
knowingly, willfully, or recklessly permitting the
guilty spouse to commit adultery. The key element of
connivance is that it must precede the adulterous event.

122   FAMILY LAW

documents has been examined, one side may demand to see certain or all documents on the list. In effect, therefore, both parties should have the same information in their possession. Once this has occurred, if the case cannot be settled out of court, a process known as an EXAMINATION FOR DISCOVERY will be arranged. An examination for discovery is a process whereby the Plaintiff's lawyer questions (examines) the Defendant in the presence of the Defendant's lawyer and a court reporter, and vice versa. The court reporter records the proceedings verbatim and produces a typewritten transcript for both parties to peruse. The purpose of an examination for discovery is to clarify the facts and issues of a case and to obtain admissions from the other party. Often the outcome of an examination for discovery is a settlement.

PARAGRAPH 5

Attempts to settle out of court are usually made by one party proposing settlement terms in the form of a WITHOUT PREJUDICE letter. A Without Prejudice letter is one that cannot be used in court as evidence. If, however, all attempts to settle out of court are fruitless, the Plaintiff arranges a trial date that is convenient to all parties and the court concerned. The Plaintiff prepares a Notice of Trial and a Trial Record (containing all the relevant documents required by the court for trial). Depending on the nature of the case, the trial may be by Judge alone or

Read the following passages carefully. Set your speed and accuracy goals and then take three-minute timings on each.

TIMING 1

When a client approaches a law firm to handle a di-	11
vorce, the divorce lawyer will try to ascertain whether	22
the client has grounds for divorce. Under the Divorce Act,	34
1985, the only ground for divorce is marriage breakdown,	45
established by means of a one-year separation, adultery, or	57
mental or physical cruelty.	62
If a client wants to apply for a divorce because of a	74
one-year separation, the divorce lawyer must determine how	86
long the spouses have been separated and whether any recon-	98
ciliations longer than ninety days have occurred. If there	110
have been any reconciliations with a duration in excess of	122
ninety days, then the separation period will have to be	133
calculated from the date of the cessation of the last	144
reconciliation.	147
If adultery (where one spouse has had sexual inter-	158
course with another person other than his or her spouse)	169
has taken place, the lawyer must ask the client whether he	181
or she has any names, dates, or places of any suspected	192
adultery or whether the adulterous spouse has admitted to	203
committing adultery.	207

· · · · 1 · · · · 2 · · · · 3 · · · · 4 · · · · 5 · · · · 6 · · · 7 · · · · 8 · · · · 9 · · · · 10 · · · · 11 · · · · 12

by Judge and jury. If the trial is by Judge alone, the Judge decides the questions of fact: who is at fault, as well as the questions of law (the compensation to be granted). If the trial is by Judge and jury, the jury decides the questions of fact and the Judge decides the questions of law. The Judge passes judgment either orally at the end of the trial or in writing, in the form of "Reasons for Judgment," after the trial.

PARAGRAPH 6

When a case goes to trial, both sides want to call witnesses to support their arguments. Generally, the lawyer calls the witnesses, either individually or as a group, to a meeting in his or her office prior to the trial. The objective of the meeting is to brief the witnesses on court procedure and to give them a dry run at their testimony. At this time, the lawyer can prepare the witnesses for the type of questions the opposing Counsel is likely to ask. From the lawyer's point of view, he or she obtains a better picture of how the witnesses will support the case and, sometimes, how well they will stand up under cross-examination. If a lawyer is dubious as to whether a witness will show up in court, he or she may issue a SUBPOENA. A Subpoena is a legal document that directs the witness to attend at court on a certain day at a certain time. If the witness does not appear in court after being served with a Subpoena, he or she is considered to be in contempt of court. The term "Subpoena" comes from the Latin and means "under penalty."

CLAUSE 5

3.   THAT the Husband shall have custody of the infant child of the marriage, namely, SANDRO PAPILE, and the Wife shall have reasonable access to the said child. In particular, and without restricting the generality of the foregoing, the Wife shall have access to the said child for a period of one week during the Christmas or Easter vacation and for a period of four weeks during the summer vacation.

CLAUSE 6

15.   The Wife shall have exclusive possession of the matrimonial home until

(a)   she marries;

(b)   she cohabits in the matrimonial home with a male person, as though they were husband and wife, for a period greater than 90 days;

(c)   no child of the marriage under the age of 16 years is ordinarily resident with her in the matrimonial home; or

(d)   she ceases to reside in the matrimonial home for a period in excess of 90 days.

3-MINUTE TIMINGS

Read the following passages carefully. Set your speed and accuracy goals and then take a three-minute timing on each.

TIMING 1

During the course of an action, it is often necessary	12
for either the Plaintiff's or Defendant's lawyer to obtain a	24
Court Order. This is likely to happen when, for example,	35
substitutional service is required or when pleadings beyond	47
the Reply stage are necessary. The process of applying for	59
a Court Order is called an "interlocutory application" or	70
abbreviated to simply "application."	77
In most jurisdictions, applications for Court Orders	88
are heard by Judges in Chambers. This means that the Judge	100
and the lawyers are not robed and the atmosphere is gener-	112
ally much more informal than that of a trial courtroom.	123
One lawyer asks the Judge for an Order and provides back-	134
ground details. The other lawyer may argue against the	145
Order. The Judge makes a decision based on what he or she	157
has heard from both parties.	163
The lawyer seeking a Court Order must contact the local	175
courthouse and arrange a Chambers hearing date. Once this	187
has been done, the lawyer prepares the necessary documen-	198
tation for the Judge, files the documents in the court,	209
and serves them on any opposing Counsel. If there is	220

· · · ·1· · · ·2· · · ·3· · · ·4· · · ·5· · · ·6· · · ·7· · · ·8· · · ·9· · · ·10· · · ·11· · · ·12

CLAUSE 3

11.5   The Husband shall:

11.5.1   keep THE FEDERATED LIFE INSURANCE COMPANY
         ("Federated") life policy in full force and effect;

11.5.2   pay all premiums, dues, and assessments payable
         under the Federated life policy; and

11.5.3   annually, within 14 days of the date any premium,
         dues, or assessment is payable under the Federated
         life policy, provide to the Wife a copy of the
         receipt for payment of such premium, dues, or
         assessment.

CLAUSE 4

7.1   On June 15, 19--, the Wife shall deliver to PRAIRIE
MOVING AND STORAGE CO. LTD. at her residence those chattels
set out in Schedule B for delivery to the Husband at his
residence.

7.2   The Husband shall be responsible for the costs of
the transfer of chattels pursuant to clause 7.1.

no opposing Counsel, as with an Order for Substitutional Service, the application is known as an "ex parte application."

The documentation for a regular application usually consists of a Notice of Motion and a supporting Affidavit. The Notice of Motion is a document that sets out the names of the parties to the case, the type of Court Order sought, the Court Rule or Act under which the Court Order is being requested, and the date and time of the hearing. The supporting Affidavit provides the Judge with the background details of the application.

The Judge hears the lawyer's application and opposing Counsel's arguments, and then pronounces a Court Order. The Judge outlines the specifics of the Order. The lawyers make notes, as does the Court Clerk. Anyone present at the Chambers hearing can prepare the Court Order; however, this is usually done by the lawyer who has obtained the Order. The prepared Order is signed by both lawyers and then sent to the court, where it is checked by the Court Clerk and signed by the court.

. . . . 1 . . . . 2 . . . . 3 . . . . 4 . . . . 5 . . . . 6 . . . . 7 . . . . 8 . . . . 9 . . . . 10 . . . . 11 12

TIMING 2 (3 min)

While the most common method of commencing a civil proceeding is by an action, there is another method called an "originating application." An originating application is used when the parties to the proceeding do not have any matter to

PARAGRAPH PRACTICE

Read the following family law Agreement clauses and then key an accurate copy of each one. If you make any errors, drill each word correctly for one minute.

CLAUSE 1

6.   THAT the Husband will pay to the Wife for the support of the infant child of the marriage, namely LILY MAN-UNG CHAU, the sum of FOUR HUNDRED AND FIFTY ($450.00) DOLLARS per month and the payment shall continue so long as the said child is in the care and control of the Wife, or until the said child attains the age of eighteen years, dies, marries, or otherwise becomes self-supporting.

CLAUSE 2

19.   Brock and Eleanor each acknowledge that he or she:

(a) has received independent legal advice; and

(b) has read this Agreement carefully, knows and understands its contents, and has executed it voluntarily, without any undue influence or coercion by the other.

dispute but the law requires a hearing in front of a Judge. The following is an example: Your grandfather set up a trust for you and your sister that paid out $1,000 per month to each of you. Your sister decided that she would like to vary this trust and obtain a lump sum payment for the down payment on a house. You are in agreement with the variation of the trust but the trust cannot be varied under law without a court hearing. This would be regarded as an originating application.

There are several major differences between an action and an originating application. One difference is that the parties to an action are called the "Plaintiff" and "Defendant," whereas the parties to an originating application are called the "Petitioner" and "Respondent." A second difference is that the initial document in an action is a Writ of Summons (or similar document), whereas the initial document in an originating application is a Petition or a Praecipe. A Petition is used when the Respondent needs to be notified of the application (as in the case of the example of the variation of a trust). A Praecipe is used when no other party needs to be notified of the application, such as an application for a name change.

When a Praecipe is used, a draft Court

Each party to a marriage must freely consent to the marriage. This means that neither party must marry under duress. Duress refers to someone exercising force (not necessarily physical) to compel another person to do something. The element of fear is important in duress. For example, for duress to be proven, a person must have frightened one of the parties to the marriage sufficiently that he or she is unable to make a voluntary choice to marry.

For a court to annul a marriage on the grounds of duress, the party's emotional stability, age, and intelligence will be taken into account. In addition, the time the duress was exercised will be examined. For example, if the time between the alleged duress and the marriage ceremony is substantial, the court may not consider a claim of duress to be valid.

	11
	22
	33
	45
	56
	68
	79
	90
	101
	113
	124
	135
	146
	157
	163

· · · ·1· · · ·2· · · ·3· · · ·4· · · ·5· · · ·6· · · ·7· · · ·8· · · ·9· · · ·10· · · ·11· · · ·12

COMPREHENSION 2

Indicate your knowledge of the following terms by using each one in a separate sentence. If you are uncertain of any words, use your dictionary.

annulment

access

duress

Petitioner

Respondent

parental consent

consanguinity

Separation Agreement

common law relationship

custody

Order and supporting Affidavits are prepared by the Petitioner's lawyer. These documents are filed in the Court Registry, a registration fee is paid, and the Judge reviews the documentation without the lawyer having to be present.

In the case of a Petition, the Petitioner's lawyer prepares supporting Affidavits and files them in the Court Registry, together with the required filing fee. He or she, however, will have to appear in front of a Judge in Chambers.

Other differences in commencing a proceeding by means of an originating application are that there are no pleadings; no lists of documents are exchanged; and no examinations for discovery are held. An originating application is usually heard before a Judge in Chambers, instead of a trial being held in a courtroom. This means that evidence is presented to the Judge by means of Affidavits rather than by witnesses.

| 305 |
| 315 |
| 325 |
| 333 |
| 341 |
| 351 |
| 360 |
| 369 |
| 378 |
| 387 |
| 397 |
| 406 |
| 415 |
| 425 |
| 435 |
| 444 |
| 453 |
| 463 |
| 471 |

TIMING 3 (3 min)

If the Defendant in an action does not file either an Appearance or a Statement of Defence, the Plaintiff is considered to have won the case by default. If either the Plaintiff or the Defendant does not show up at the trial, again the other party is considered to have won by default. If the Defendant defaults, he or she is expected to pay the

| 12 |
| 23 |
| 35 |
| 46 |
| 58 |
| 70 |

. . . . 1 . . . . 2 . . . . 3 . . . . 4 . . . . 5 . . . . 6 . . . . 7 . . . . 8 . . . . 9 . . . . 10 . . . . 11 12

Columbia, Newfoundland, and Nova Scotia, where the age is 19. In most provinces, individuals aged between 16 and 18 may marry, provided they have parental consent.

159
168
177
180

TIMING 3

Two people who have close blood ties (consanguinity) usually cannot marry. Each province has its own list of forbidden marriages; however, the following is representative of most provincial Marriage Acts.

A woman cannot marry her grandfather, grandmother's husband, husband's grandfather, uncle, husband's uncle, father, stepfather, husband's father, son, husband's son, daughter's husband, brother, grandson, granddaughter's husband, husband's grandson, nephew, or niece's husband.

A man is subject to the same restrictions but, of course, for the opposite gender. For example, he cannot marry his grandmother, grandfather's wife, etc.

If any marriage between the above parties does take place, the marriage is void and an annulment can be applied for and obtained.

The federal Marriage Act allows a woman to marry her husband's brother or nephew, provided that her husband is dead. Conversely, a man can marry his wife's sister or niece, provided that his wife is not alive.

11
22
33
41
52
63
74
85
96
107
118
127
138
150
153
164
175
186
195

· · · ·1· · · ·2· · · ·3· · · ·4· · · ·5· · · ·6· · · ·7· · · ·8· · · ·9· · · ·10· · · ·11· · · ·12

Plaintiff the damages listed in the Default Judgment.

If a case goes to trial, the loser will have to pay the proven damages as well as costs. The costs normally include a portion of the successful party's legal fees, court filing fees, transcript expenses, etc. Legal fees are known as "solicitor-client costs" and should not be confused with court costs, which are the filing fees, transcript expenses, etc.

Each province has Court Rules that include schedules of fees. These schedules are used by the successful lawyer to prepare a Bill of Costs. The party who wins the case cannot expect that all of his or her legal fees will be paid. Generally speaking, the successful party can expect to recover approximately one-half to two-thirds of his or her legal fees.

When the successful party's lawyer has prepared a Bill of Costs, a copy is sent to the unsuccessful party's lawyer. If the latter disagrees with the Bill of Costs, he or she can take the matter before the Registrar/Taxing Officer. This process is known as "taxation" of the Bill of Costs. The Registrar/Taxing Officer reviews the Bill of Costs and compares the charges to the schedules of fees in the Court Rules. If necessary, the Registrar/Taxing Officer will reduce the amount of the Bill of Costs.

If the Defendant loses the case, in addition to costs, he or she will also have to pay damages (compensation for injuries suffered). Damages fall into several categories.

. . . . 1 . . . . 2 . . . . 3 . . . . 4 . . . . 5 . . . 6 . . . . 7 . . . . 8 . . . 9 . . . . 10 . . . . 11 . . . 12

Occasionally the federal government has not enacted specific marriage laws and the provincial governments have stepped in and made their own statutes, although they are not officially entitled to do so. One example is that the federal Marriage Act does not include a list of persons who may not marry because they are too closely related. Most provincial governments have, therefore, composed this list and included it in their Marriage Acts.

90
102
113
125
137
148
160
168

· · · ·1· · · ·2· · · ·3· · · ·4· · · ·5· · · ·6· · · ·7· · · ·8· · · ·9· · · ·10· · · ·11· · · ·12

TIMING 2

Several conditions should exist for a marriage to be considered lawful. These conditions include that the parties to the marriage be free to marry (not already married), of marriageable age, mentally competent (of sound mind), sexually capable (able to perform sexual intercourse), and free from duress or threats. The parties must also understand that they are participating in a marriage ceremony. Failure to meet any of these requirements does not mean that the marriage is invalid; however, grounds for divorce or annulment of the marriage may exist.

Each province has its own minimum age requirements for marriage, both with and without parental consent. Most provinces allow marriage at age 18 without parental consent, except British

11
22
33
43
53
64
73
83
93
102
111
119
129
139
149

Special damages relate to tangible expenses, such as medi- |370|
cal costs, loss of wages, and property damage. General |381|
damages relate to intangibles, such as loss of personal |392|
happiness due to injury, pain, and suffering. Nominal |403|
damages refer to a small amount of money being given to the |415|
Plaintiff to show good faith, even though the Plaintiff |426|
suffered minimal injury. Punitive damages refer to com- |437|
pensation for obnoxious behaviour toward the Plaintiff. |448|

. . . .1. . . .2. . . .3. . . .4. . . .5. . . 6. . . .7. . . .8. . . .9. . . .10. . . .11. . . .12

COMPREHENSION 3

Read the following sentences carefully. Key each sentence once, correcting all errors in fact, terminology, spelling, grammar, and punctuation. Use your dictionary and office handbook.

1. A Writ at Summons stipulates the length of time the the Defendent has to advice the Plaintiff that he or she wants to defend the action.

2. The lawyer, filed an appearance, in court one behalf of her client.

3. The Plainitiff's lawyer prepares the Statement of Claims.

4. If the Defendent fails to file either an Appearance for a Statement of Defence within the set limitation period, the Plainitiff can prepare a Default Judgement.

9. The parent who is granted custody of the children of the marriage is responsible for the care and upbringing of the children.

10. Access refers to the right of the non-custodial parent to visit the children of the marriage.

11. The term "family assets" (or "family property") refers to property owned by one or both spouses that is used by the family (e.g., cars, boats, summer cottages, furniture, etc.).

12. The party suing for divorce is called the Petitioner; the party being sued is called the Respondent.

2-MINUTE TIMINGS

Read the following passages carefully. Set your speed and accuracy goals. Take two-minute timings on each passage.

TIMING 1

While the federal government enacts laws relating to	11
marriage, the provincial governments enact laws concerning	23
the administration of a marriage. For example, the federal	35
government can enact laws relating to a valid marriage, such	47
as requiring that both parties be of sound mind, whereas	58
a provincial government can enact laws relating to how,	69
when, and where Marriage Licences can be obtained.	79

· · · ·1· · · ·2· · · ·3· · · ·4· · · ·5· · · ·6· · · ·7· · · ·8· · · ·9· · · ·10· · · ·11· · · ·12

5. Pleadings are the set od documents prepared by both sides that present the facts and issues of the case.

6. Examples of pleadings are: Rejoiner, Surrejoiner, Rebutter, and Surrebutter

7. The Court Reporter recorded the proceedings of the examination for discovery.

8. If the trial is by Judge and jury, the jury will decides the questions of law.

9. A Subpoena is a legal document that directs a witness to attend at court on a certain day at a certain time.

10. The prosess of applying for a Court Order is called an "interloctutory application."

11. A civil proceeding can be commenced by either an action or an originating application.

12. The first document in an action is a Petition or Preacipe.

Check your accuracy with your instructor. If you made any errors in spelling or terminology, drill each word for one minute.

SENTENCE PRACTICE

Read the following sentences carefully. Key each sentence once. Concentrate on accuracy and rhythmic keying.

1. A Pre-Nuptial Agreement (or Marriage Contract) is an Agreement (usually regarding property) made between a couple prior to their marriage.

2. A Marriage Licence or special permit must be obtained before a marriage ceremony takes place.

3. If a marriage is not consummated (the couple does not have sexual intercourse), the marriage may be declared null.

4. Annulment is a legal term that means that a marriage is no longer valid and never was valid in the eyes of the law.

5. A Cohabitation Agreement is a domestic Agreement between two or more people who live together.

6. A common law relationship exists when a man and woman live together but they are not married or their marriage is not recognized under Canadian law.

7. A Separation Agreement may be drawn up between a husband and wife when they have separated.

8. A Separation Agreement may include clauses relating to custody of children, access rights, spousal or child maintenance, and division of family assets.

5- OR 10-MINUTE TIMINGS

Read the following passages carefully. Set your speed and accuracy goals and then take either five- or ten-minute timings.

TIMING 1

Often a Court Order will stipulate that one party must	12
pay the other party a certain sum of money. Sometimes it	24
will stipulate that certain goods have to be returned.	35
Whatever the circumstances, the person who is required to	46
pay the money or return the goods is called the "Judgment	58
Debtor." The party who is trying to obtain the money or	69
goods is called the "Judgment Creditor." If the Judgment	80
Debtor does not pay the money or return the goods within a	92
specified time limit, then the Judgment Creditor will take	104
other steps to satisfy the terms of the Order. This process	116
is called "collection."	121
The first step in the collection process is for the	132
Judgment Creditor to obtain some information on the Judgment	144
Debtor. This information might include details of the	155
Judgment Debtor's real property (home) and personal property	167
(car, boat, motor home, etc.). The information can be	178
obtained by the Judgment Creditor's lawyer conducting	189
searches in various government agencies; for example, Land	201
Title Offices, Motor Vehicle Registries/Departments, etc.	212
Alternatively, the Judgment Creditor's lawyer can obtain	223
the information by questioning the Judgment Debtor in an	234

. . . . 1 . . . . 2 . . . . 3 . . . . 4 . . . . 5 . . . . 6 . . . . 7 . . . . 8 . . . . 9 . . . . 10 . . . . 11 . . . 12

account. Support is for the relief of economic hardship: it is not a form of court-ordered punishment.

Did you achieve your speed and accuracy goals on at least one of the timings? If not, repeat the timings.

COMPREHENSION 1

Key the following sentences once, filling in each blank with the appropriate legal term or phrase.

1. --- is for the relief of economic hardship following divorce.

2. Either --- can apply for a divorce.

3. If a couple --- for more than ninety days during a one-year separation, they cannot apply for a divorce.

4. Under --- Act, --- is the only grounds for divorce.

5. Most family matters, with the exception of ---, are governed by provincial laws.

6. Family law covers --- divorces and --- divorces.

Check your answers with your instructor.

examination in aid of execution (similar to an examination for discovery). If the Judgment Creditor's lawyer wants to question the Judgment Debtor in court, a Subpoena must be prepared and issued.

Once the Judgment Creditor's lawyer has obtained sufficient information on the Judgment Debtor's financial situation, he or she can take the next step in the collection process. This step is meant to force the Judgment Debtor to pay the money or deliver the goods. This can be done by a Garnishing Order, a Certificate of Judgment, or one of a series of Writs of Execution.

A Garnishing Order is used when the Judgment Creditor's lawyer discovers that the Judgment Debtor has some source of income, either from employment or debts he or she is owed. The idea behind a Garnishing Order is that the money that would have gone to the Judgment Debtor is diverted into court and the Judgment Creditor's lawyer then applies to the court to have the money paid out to the Judgment Creditor. If this sounds complicated, the following is an example.

Imagine that you are the Judgment Debtor, that you have a job, and that you owe the Judgment Creditor $20,000. The Judgment Creditor prepares a Garnishing Order that orders your employer to pay a portion of your wages into court each payday. The Judgment Creditor then applies to the court for payment out of your garnished wages.

If the Judgment Creditor's lawyer discovers that the Judgment Debtor has real property, he or she places a

· · · · 1 · · · · 2 · · · · 3 · · · · 4 · · · · 5 · · · · 6 · · · · 7 · · · · 8 · · · · 9 · · · · 10 · · · · 11 · · · · 12

TIMING 3

Under the Divorce Act, 1985, marriage breakdown is the only | 12
ground for divorce. Marriage breakdown in legal terms is | 23
defined as one-year separation, adultery, or mental/physical | 35
cruelty. If any of these situations exist, then either the | 47
husband or the wife (or both) can apply to the courts for | 58
a divorce. | 60

. . . .1. . . .2. . . .3. . . .4. . . .5. . . .6. . . .7. . . .8. . . .9. . . .10. . . .11. . . .12

TIMING 4

Either spouse can apply for a divorce based on separation | 11
before the one-year separation period has expired; however, | 23
the couple must have lived separate and apart for one year | 35
by the time the divorce hearing takes place. If a couple | 46
reconciles for more than ninety days during a one-year | 57
separation, they cannot apply for a divorce until one year | 69
from the separation date following reconciliation. | 79

. . . .1. . . .2. . . .3. . . .4. . . .5. . . .6. . . .7. . . .8. . . .9. . . .10. . . .11. . . .12

TIMING 5

While provincial laws govern the division of property, | 11
the Divorce Act has jurisdiction over which spouse | 21
should pay the other financial support following a | 31
divorce. When a Judge decides whether to award | 41
support, economic considerations are taken into | 50

Certificate of Judgment (which is a charge or encumbrance) |541|
against the property. This means that the Judgment Debtor |553|
cannot sell his or her house until the Judgment Creditor is |565|
paid. Once payment is made, the Certificate of Judgment |576|
will be cancelled. |580|

Writs of Execution are used if the Judgment Creditor's |592|
lawyer wants to have the Sheriff act on his or her behalf in |604|
seizing property. Examples of Writs of Execution are Writ |616|
of Possession, Writ of Delivery, and Writ of Seizure and |627|
Sale. |628|

· · · ·1· · · ·2· · · ·3· · · ·4· · · ·5· · · ·6· · · ·7· · · ·8· · · ·9· · · ·10· · · ·11· · · ·12

TIMING 2 (5 or 10 min)

Torts can be either intentional torts or negligence. |11|
An intentional tort is one in which the Tortfeasor is |22|
certain of the results of his or her action, wants to commit |34|
the act, and uses voluntary movement to perform the act. |45|
Examples of intentional torts are assault, battery, false |56|
imprisonment, infliction of mental suffering, interference |67|
with land (trespass and nuisance), and interference with |78|
chattels. |80|

Assault and battery are two distinct torts. Assault |91|
occurs when the victim believes that he or she is about to |103|
be physically harmed against his or her will, but no physi- |115|
cal contact takes place. Battery, on the other hand, |126|
occurs when the victim is touched; for example, kicked, |137|
punched, slapped, or stabbed. The victim, however, does not |149|

· · · ·1· · · ·2· · · ·3· · · ·4· · · ·5· · · ·6· · · ·7· · · ·8· · · ·9· · · ·10· · · ·11· · · ·12

1-MINUTE TIMINGS

Read the following paragraphs carefully. Set your speed and accuracy goals. Take one-minute timings on each paragraph.

TIMING 1

Family law covers a wide range of topics, including mar- | 11
riage; Pre-Nuptial Agreements (Marriage Contracts); matrimo- | 23
nial property; domestic Contracts (Cohabitation Agreements); | 35
separation; Separation Agreements; divorce mediation; | 46
undefended and defended divorces; name changes; child | 57
support, access, custody, and guardianship; childnapping; | 68
child abuse; and adoption. | 73

. . . .1. . . .2. . . .3. . . .4. . . .5. . . .6. . . .7. . . .8. . . .9. . . .10. . . .11. . . .12

TIMING 2

Most family matters are governed by provincial laws. The | 11
exception to this is divorce, which is governed by a federal | 23
law called the Divorce Act. The names of the provincial | 34
Acts dealing with family matters vary from province to | 45
province; however, the name of the Act usually indicates its | 57
content (e.g., Marriage Act, Family Relations Act, Change of | 69
Name Act). | 71

. . . .1. . . .2. . . .3. . . .4. . . .5. . . .6. . . .7. . . .8. . . .9. . . .10. . . .11. . . .12

have to be injured for battery to have occurred. If the battery is offensive to the victim, even if there is no injury, the victim can claim nominal damages.

Assault can be both an intentional tort and a criminal offence. As an intentional tort, assault may be the basis for a civil action initiated by an individual. As a criminal offence, assault may be the basis for a criminal prosecution by the Crown.

False imprisonment as an intentional tort refers to the victim being prevented from leaving a place. This could be preventing someone from getting out of a car or leaving a room. False arrest also constitutes false imprisonment. False imprisonment cannot be claimed if the victim has other ways of getting away from his or her confinement.

Infliction of mental suffering is an intentional tort if the Defendant causes the victim severe emotional distress through his or her extreme conduct. There have been cases where a witness has brought a claim against a Defendant for infliction of mental suffering. These witnesses were either close family members of the victim or were strangers who were both physically and mentally injured.

Two kinds of interference with land come under the heading of intentional torts: trespass and nuisance. Trespass is the unauthorized entry onto another person's land or some type of interference with the owner's or renter's enjoyment of the land. Trespass can be either intentional or unintentional.

WORD PRACTICE

Key one line of each of the following words. Concentrate on accuracy and rhythmic keying.

maintenance	matrimonial
marriage	support
affinity	defended
reconciliation	consanguinity
access	undefended
collusion	connivance
custody	null
divorce	adultery
condonation	cohabitation
spouse	separation

PHRASE PRACTICE

Key each of the following phrases six times. Concentrate on accuracy. Say each phrase to yourself as you key it. Remember to key rhythmically.

null and void	resumption of cohabitation
defended divorce	common law relationship
Pre-Nuptial Agreement	custody and access
matrimonial home	Separation Agreement
family assets	support and maintenance

Nuisance, on the other hand, refers to something that the Defendant does to damage the Plaintiff's land or something that the Defendant does that destroys the Plaintiff's "quiet enjoyment" of his or her land. Examples of nuisance are: noise, dirt, smells, radio transmissions, etc., which relate to private nuisance. There is a category of public nuisance that refers to someone annoying the general public. Creating a public nuisance is a criminal offence and does not come under the category of civil law.

Interference with chattels relates to moving or interferring with objects (cars, boats, etc.) belonging to other people, without the owners' permission. If the chattels are damaged, the Defendant must pay for the cost of the goods. If the chattels are not damaged, the Defendant will be liable for either nominal damages or no damages at all.

One major difference between an intentional tort and negligence is that the Plaintiff in an intentional tort case does not have to prove actual damage, whereas the Plaintiff in a negligence case must prove that he or she suffered damage, that the conduct of the Defendant (Tortfeasor) was the cause of the damage, and that the Defendant had a duty in law to avoid the particular conduct but he or she breached that duty.

Many negligence cases revolve around the concept of a "reasonable person." This is the standard that the court uses to determine whether the Defendant's conduct was negligent. Unfortunately, very few people could live up to the

. . . . 1 . . . . 2 . . . . 3 . . . . 4 . . . . 5 . . . . 6 . . . . 7 . . . . 8 . . . . 9 . . . . 10 . . . . 11 12

Family Law

standard of a "reasonable person." A "reasonable person" | 756 |
is always diligent, always aware of potential risks, and | 767 |
always thinking of the welfare of others. In other words, | 779 |
if you were a "reasonable person" you probably wouldn't ever | 791 |
leave home for fear of putting yourself into a situation | 802 |
where you could be accused of being negligent! | 811 |

. . . .1 . . . .2 . . . .3 . . . .4 . . . .5 . . . .6 . . . .7 . . . .8 . . . .9 . . . .10 . . . .11 12

TIMING 3 (5 or 10 min)

There are two main categories of Contracts : simple | 11 |
and speciality. Simple Contracts are in verbal, | 21 |
written, or implied form but they do not have | 30 |
to follow any prescribed wording or be signed | 39 |
under seal. Specialty Contracts are in written | 48 |
form and are signed under seal. Examples of | 57 |
specialty Contracts are Mortgages, Leases, Licensing | 67 |
Agreements, Separation Agreements, and Service | 76 |
Contracts. | 78 |

To sign under seal means that the parties | 87 |
to the Contract sign their names and a red seal | 96 |
is placed at the end of the signature line. | 105 |
Instead of a seal, the word "seal" or the | 113 |
letters "L.S." (locus sigilli: place for the seal) | 123 |
can be placed at the end of the signature line. | 132 |

There are certain requirements for a Contract | 142 |
to be valid; for example, offer and acceptance. | 151 |
For a Contract to be valid, someone must offer | 160 |

NO.   REGISTER

IN THE   COURT OF

BETWEEN:

PLAINTIFF(S),

AND:

DEFENDANT(S).

WRIT OF SUMMONS

Tel: (   )

File No.

to make a Contract (the Offeror) and someone else must accept the offer (the Offeree).

The elements of a proper offer are that it must be definite, intended, and communicated to the Offeree. If the Offeree wants to accept the offer and form a Contract, then he or she must communicate acceptance of the offer to the Offeror in accordance with the manner and within the time frame stated in the offer. The Offeree's acceptance must be unconditional.

An offer can be revoked (cancelled) by the Offeror withdrawing the offer. There are, however, circumstances under which an offer is automatically revoked: (a) a counter-offer is made; (b) the Offeror dies before the Offeree has accepted the offer; and (c) the Offeree does not accept the offer within the time frame stated in the offer.

Once an offer has been made and accepted, a Contract is drawn up and signed by all parties to the Contract. One of the essential elements of a simple Contract is that it must state some consideration (value). If no consideration is stipulated, then in the eyes of the law one party is doing something for the other party free of charge. There is no Contract per se, merely a gift. Contracts under seal do not need to state a consideration.

ENDORSEMENT

The Plaintiffs' claim is:

Dated this   day of   , 19 .

_____
Solicitor for the Plaintiff(s)

TIME FOR APPEARANCE

Where this Writ is served on a person in   ,
the time for appearance by that person is 7 days from the
service (not including the day of service).

Where this Writ is served on a person outside   ,
the time for appearance by that person, after service, shall
be 21 days in the case of a person residing anywhere within
Canada, 28 days in the case of a person residing in the
United States of America, and 42 days in the case of a
person residing elsewhere. The Court may shorten the time
for appearance on ex parte application.

The parties to a Contract must have the legal capacity to make a Contract. Minors can make certain Contracts with adults but generally they are permitted to cancel these Contracts without any penalty. There are certain categories of people who cannot make Contracts: mentally incompetent people and people who are under the influence of alcohol and/or drugs.

If a person makes a Contract while he or she is intoxicated, the Contract can be revoked if three points can be proven: the person was actually intoxicated to the extent that he or she did not know that a Contract was being made; the other parties to the Contract were aware that the person was intoxicated; and the person sought to revoke the Contract within a reasonable time of it being made (for example, when he or she sobered up).

Besides the parties to a Contract having the legal capacity to make a Contract, they must also consent to make the Contract. If any party is forced to sign a Contract under duress or undue influence, the Contract is invalid. "Duress" means that someone has forced one of the parties to sign the Contract. This force may be in the form of threats to the person's life or well-being. Undue influence is when someone coerces one of the

YOU OR YOUR SOLICITOR may file the "Appearance". You may obtain a form of "Appearance" at the Registry.

IF YOU FAIL to file the "Appearance" within the proper Time for Appearance, JUDGMENT MAY BE TAKEN AGAINST YOU without further notice.

THE ADDRESS OF THE REGISTRY IS:

Name and office of Plaintiffs' solicitor (if any):

Plaintiffs' address for delivery:

parties to sign a Contract even though the party does not want to sign.

A Contract can also be voided (have no legal force) if there is a serious mistake or genuine misunderstanding in the terms of the Contract or if there has been any misrepresentation (false or misleading words or actions).

| 655 |
| 661 |
| 671 |
| 680 |
| 690 |
| 700 |
| 706 |

PRODUCTION EXERCISES

EXERCISE 1

When keying Court Orders, you need to know the correct form of address for a Judge. In addition, you need to know how to refer to various other parties who appeared at the trial or hearing, because this information is used in the preamble (first part) of a Court Order.

Read the following information carefully, watching for errors. Set yourself a production time limit. Key the material as two boxed tables. Provide appropriate main headings for each of the tables, as well as column headings. Key your work quickly and accurately.

Table 1:

Chief Justice of (Name of Province): The Honourable, The Chief Justice (Name)

Chief Justice of the Supreme Court: The Honourable, The Chief Justice (Name)

Supreme Court Judge: The Honourable Mr. Justice (Name) or The Honouourable Madam Justice (Name)

2.

ELIZABETH THE SECOND, by the Grace of God, of the United Kingdom, Canada and Her other Realms and Territories, Queen, Head of the Commonwealth, Defender of the Faith.

TO THE DEFENDANT(S):

TAKE NOTICE that this action has been commenced against you by the Plaintiff(s) for the claim(s) set out in this Writ.

IF YOU INTEND TO DEFEND this action, or if you have a set-off or counterclaim which you wish to have taken into account at the trial, YOU MUST GIVE NOTICE of your intention by filing a form entitled "Appearance" in the above Registry of this Court within the Time for Appearance endorsed hereon and YOU MUST ALSO DELIVER a copy of the "Appearance" to the Plaintiffs' address for delivery, which is set out in this Writ.

County Court Judge in Supreme Court: The Honourable Judge (Name), a Local Judge of the Supreme Court

County Court Judge in Country Court: The Honourable Judge (Name)

Adapted from Evin Ross. *Guide to Civil Litigation*. BC edition. Delta, BC: Evin Ross Publications Ltd., p. 223.

Table 2:

Solicitor of Record: Wafa Sheleb, Esq., Solicitor for the (Plaintiff, Defendant, etc.) / Maureen MacLean, Solicitor for the (Plaintiff, Defendant, etc.)

Another lawyer acting as Counsel for the Solicitor of Record: David Muis, Esq., Counsel for the (Plaintiff, Defendent, etc.) / Sara Shao, Counsel for the (Plaintiff, Defendant, etc.)

Articling student appearing for Solicitor or Council: Charan Sethi, Esq., Articled student on behalf of Solicitor/Counsel for the (Plaintiff/Defendant, etc.) / Lynda Fletcher, Articled student on behalf of Solicitor/Counsel for the (Plaintiff/Defendant, etc.)

Party appearing on own behalf: Nathan Gold, appearing on his own behalf / June Vanduyn, appearing on his own behalf

No-show (party does not show up although served either personnally or through lawyer): No-one appearing on behalf of (Name), although duly served (or delivered)

Adapted from Evin Ross. *Guide to Civil Litigation*. BC edition. Delta, BC: Evin Ross Publications Ltd., p. 224.

Read the following precedent Writ of Summons carefully. Make sure that you understand the material. Set yourself a production time limit. Key the Writ quickly and accurately, adapting the precedent to apply to situations involving one Plaintiff and one Defendant.

                                        NO.
                                              REGISTER

        IN THE   COURT OF

BETWEEN:

                                        PLAINTIFF(S),
    AND:

                                        DEFENDANT(S).

            WRIT OF SUMMONS
(Name and address of each Plaintiff)

(Name and address of each Defendant)

Read the following precedent Writ of Seizure and Sale carefully. Check the document for content and formatting accuracy. Prepare the backing sheet in landscape mode. Use the same lawyer and law firm name as shown in the backing sheet example on page 63. Set yourself a production time limit and then key the material quickly and accurately.

```
                                      NO.    REGISTRY


         IN THE                   COURT OF


BETWEEN:




                                           PLAINTIFF(S),
                                           APPLICANT(S),


AND:




                                           DEFENDANT(S).
                                           RESPONDENT(S).


              WRIT OF SIEZURE AND SALE


TO THE SHERRIFF:

         You are commended forthwith to seize and sell at
public auction or by tender for the best available price
sufficient of the goods and chattles of the undermentioned
person to realize the sums set out on the back of this Writ,
```

NO.   REGISTRY

IN THE

COURT OF

BETWEEN:

PLAINTIFF(S),
APPLICANT(S),

AND:

DEFENDANT(S).
RESPONDENTS.

WRIT OF SEIZURE AND SALE

File No.   /

which are payable by virtue of the attached Order of this Honourable Court, together with your costs, fees, and expenses for executing this Write.

After carrying out the above instructions you shall pay to the person specified on the back of this Writ from the amount realized the sum or sums that are payable to him and account therefor by return to the Court.

Dated this   day of   , 19 .

_____
District Registrar

Name and address of Solicitor or person causing this Writ to be issued:

Name and address of person whose goods and chattles are to
be seized:

Amount remaining due and payable on Judgment: $

Amount of costs remaining due on payable: $

Amount of interest on Judgment and costs
remaining due and payable: $

Costs of party entitled to execution: $

Sherriff's costs: (To be completed by
Sherriff) $
_____

Total: (To be completed by Sherriff) $

Identity of person entitled to payment of Judgement: